Recollections of Anaïs Nin

RECOLLECTIONS OF

Anaïs Nin

Edited by

Benjamin Franklin V

Ohio University Press
Athens

Library of Congress Cataloging-in-Publication Data

Recollections of Anaïs Nin by her contemporaries / edited by Benjamin
Franklin V.
    p.   cm.
    Includes bibliographical references (p.).
    ISBN 0-8214-1164-0 (cloth : alk. paper). — ISBN 0-8214-1165-9
(paper : alk. paper)
    1. Nin, Anaïs, 1903-1977—Biography.   2. Nin, Anaïs, 1903-1977—
Contemporaries.   3. Women authors, American—20th century—
Biography.   I. Franklin, Benjamin, 1939-
PS3527.I865Z85   1996
818'.5209—dc20   96-15051
[B]   CIP

Ohio University Press, Athens, Ohio 45701
© 1996 by Ohio University Press
Printed in the United States of America

Ohio University Press books are printed on acid-free paper ∞

01 00 99 98 97 96   5 4 3 2 1

Portions of the essay by Rochelle Lynn Holt first appeared in *Independent Press*, February 9, 1977, published in Birmingham, Alabama,
and in Barry Donald Jones's thesis at Dartmouth College.

The poem "Thinking of Anaïs Nin" by William Claire was first published in *The Nation Magazine*, March 29, 1971, p. 414. Reprinted by
permission.

Selection from *Kafka Was the Rage* © 1993 by Anatole Broyard; reprinted
by permission of Crown Publishers, Inc.

Dedication

To JO, ABIGAIL, REBECCA, and my MOTHER

the women in my life

And to the memory of Anaïs Nin

Contents

Contents

Preface

Anaïs Nin is much with us. There is the Nin who inspired the naming of a perfume (Anaïs Anaïs); whose name is the answer to questions in crossword puzzles; who appears (as played by Maria de Medeiros) as one of the major characters in the Hollywood movie *Henry and June* (1990); who has become even more notorious than previously as a result of her depiction in *Incest* (1992) of her apparent sexual relationship, as an adult, with her father; whose psychological fiction remains in print, as does her *Diary*, with new volumes continuing to appear; whose work receives the attention of literary critics; and who is the subject of two substantial biographies in English, the first of which became a Book-of-the-Month-Club selection. Clearly, she generates interest, and probably more now, almost two decades after her death, than during her lifetime, the last years of which brought her considerable acclaim.

Nin engendered strong responses in people. Many not only admired but also idolized her; others viewed her skeptically. Some became acolytes, only to have the nature of the relationship change for one reason or another, possibly because they came to see her as merely mortal the closer they came to her and the more clearly they saw her, as was the case with me. Various responses to her appear in the recollections gathered in this book.

I compiled these recollections to permit people who knew Anaïs to relate their honest, accurate impressions — I did not try to influence what anyone wrote — of this woman all of us would agree was extraordinary, in one way or another. And so they have done. Included here are the recollections of people who knew her in varying degrees of intimacy: from a niece to students to friends to critics to people who met her only once and do not claim to have known her well. Some of the contributors knew her as far back as the 1940s, while others met her only a few years before her death in 1977. Although some of us share similar recollections of Anaïs (and some comment on the same events), consensus emerges primarily concerning her death: those in a position to know attest that she confronted her final illness and death exemplarily, magnificently.

I have generally attempted to arrange the recollections chronologically according to date of first meeting with Anaïs, with one notable exception. I have placed last the second piece by Deena Metzger, which deals solely with Anaïs's dying, even though she met Anaïs in 1965.

I first discussed *Recollections of Anaïs Nin* with Duane Schneider, then director of the Ohio University Press, in May 1994 at a Nin conference, organized by Suzanne Nalbantian, held at the Southampton campus of Long Island University. Although several of the conference participants have contributed to this book, I respect the wish of one of them in particular — Joaquín Nin-Culmell, Nin's surviving brother — not to participate in this project. With all matters concerning Nin, I am most indebted to Duane, primarily for reasons detailed in my recollection, but also for assuming some of my editorial duties while I was teaching at the University of Helsinki, Finland, during the 1995 spring semester. I am grateful to the contributors for meeting my short deadline and for having answered my bothersome questions with unfailing good humor. Some of them recommended other possible contributors, as did Deirdre Bair.

Benjamin Franklin V
Columbia, South Carolina

GAYLE NIN ROSENKRANTZ

Anaïs Nin was my aunt. My father, Thorvald Nin, was her younger brother. I have to start out with a statement of what my aunt was not. I have had several aunts, my mother's sisters, my stepmother's sisters, my father's maternal aunts, even friends referred to as "aunt," and most of these women were warm, loving, nurturing, caring individuals who were interested in me and my brother, who talked to us, asked us questions, joked with us, gave us presents, helped out on occasion with parental responsibilities. We used to stay at their homes and felt we could count on them. I always felt that my presence was a delight to these women.

My aunt was not that kind of aunt. She wasn't cross or hostile, but she wasn't interested in us. She seemed completely wrapped up in herself.

My earliest memories of Aunt Anaïs are of an exotic looking, strangely dressed woman talking with a funny accent which she claimed was French, but which my dad said was phony. I suspect she had a speech impediment which made it difficult for her to pronounce her *r*'s. It was sometime between December 1943 and May 1944, which was the period of time when my family lived in New York. We had lived in Colombia before that, and moved to Mexico afterwards. There were family dinners at our apartment in New York, and the subject of conversation would be my aunt's books, how she had to print them herself, how she and her husband had lived on a houseboat. Unusual! Perhaps the adults talked about other interests, such as the progress of the war, my uncle's

1

musical career, my father's business career, or news about cousins in Cuba, but all I can remember is my aunt talking about herself. Her husband Hugo (Hugh Guiler) also had artistic interests, although he was a banker in real life. He did copper engravings, and many of Anaïs's books were illustrated with engravings of his, under the name of Ian Hugo. We never could make heads or tails out of Hugo's engravings. However, Hugo created some copper objects which he gave to me and my brother as gifts. He seemed to relate to us more as an uncle. He talked to us and asked us questions.

Actually, I had a hard time making sense out of my aunt's writings when I was a child. I was eleven when we were living in New York, where I read the stories in *Under a Glass Bell* and *House of Incest*. It wasn't exactly Nancy Drew or *Little Women*, but I plodded through them. I think my parents didn't know I was reading those books.

We moved to Mexico in May or June of 1944, and in September of 1945 I was enrolled at Westover, a girls' boarding school in Connecticut. The decision to send me to Westover was made at the last minute. My mother sent a telegram to Aunt Anaïs in New York asking her if she would meet my plane at La Guardia, house me for a few days in New York, and then put me on the train to Westover. We never received a response, so a college friend of my mother filled in as aunt and took care of things for me. I never heard what happened to Anaïs. Perhaps she was out of town.

During Christmas vacation of 1945, I did not stay with Anaïs and Hugo. I don't know if my mother considered the possibility, or if she decided against it. She never said anything to me about it, and I didn't think about it. Only now, after all these years and some reflection, it occurs to me that it might have been natural for me to spend Christmas vacation with my aunt and uncle, but the fact is, it wasn't natural. Anaïs and Hugo didn't look after young nieces. I stayed with several friends of my mother, so that I would not stay too long with anyone. And so it went from September of 1945 until June of 1949. Whenever I spent time in New York during holidays from school, I never saw Anaïs, and nobody mentioned the possibility of visiting or saying hello. When I graduated from Westover I received many prizes and honors, and friends and relatives sent me congratulations and gifts. My father, brother, and I also spent a few days in New York before going back to Mexico. I never heard a word from Anaïs. Who knows where she was?

I think that Anaïs came to Mexico during the summer of 1950 and perhaps another time when I was a student at Stanford but home in Mexico during vacation. She was just the same as in New York. Her dress was a bit odd, more exotic than we were used to. She talked about herself a lot, and her face was strange. It was obvious she had had plastic surgery, and I couldn't keep from staring at her. After all, she was supposed to be older than my dad and she looked much younger! A boyfriend of mine met her and said he saw her at the beach in Acapulco. He said she was "well preserved," which made me think of pickles or formaldehyde. During the 1950 visit she talked about a recent trip to Brazil, and she gave me some tourmaline jewelry.

I did not see Anaïs again for years after that. I was married in the fall of 1951 and lived in California. I heard nothing from my aunt. My husband, David, graduated from Stanford Business School, then went to work for Macy's in San Francisco. In 1956 he became a buyer and made his first buying trip to New York. For some reason, I suggested that he call Anaïs and Hugo when he arrived. He did, and they invited him to dinner at the apartment in Greenwich Village. After dinner, Anaïs suggested to David that they go to a movie together; they went, and during the movie she held David's hand. When I heard about that, I was half amused and half irritated. David was twenty-six and my aunt was fifty-three at the time. David visited Anaïs and Hugo one more time after that first buying trip, but he developed friends of his own over the years and didn't see them again in New York.

In the 1960s David ran into Anaïs on an airplane flight from New York to Los Angeles. They sat together during the flight, but as soon as they arrived in Los Angeles she quickly disappeared. From a distance, David saw her being greeted by a man with two dogs.

In May of 1971, the new Roman Catholic Cathedral in San Francisco, St. Mary's, was inaugurated with a solemn Dedication Mass. My uncle Joaquín had been commissioned to compose the music for the Mass, so both my father and Aunt Anaïs came to San Francisco for this important occasion. Tickets were hard to come by, but my uncle obtained them for all of us. My parents stayed with my uncle in Berkeley, and my aunt flew up from Los Angeles just for the day. Some young admirer of hers picked her up at the airport and she showed up at the Cathedral just in time to sit down with the rest of us. Anaïs was sixty-eight years old at the time, but she showed up with her hair dyed a light reddish hue, wearing a short skirt, go-go boots, and a flowing cape which gave her a part bohemian, part hippie, part Madame Bovary look.

After the Mass, we all went to dinner at Trader Vic's. My aunt, my uncle, and my father sat next to each other, and Anaïs looked like their daughter, not their older sister. My father and my aunt were at each other's throats. My father was furious because my aunt had included mention of my father in her published diaries without his consent. The hostility between them spoiled the dinner, and my husband drove Anaïs to the airport early in the evening. I had a brief conversation with her before she left. Anaïs had said that her work required her to spend six months of the year in Los Angeles and the other six months in New York. I told Anaïs that my law practice required me to go to Los Angeles at least once a month, and I would love to see her on one of my trips. I asked for her telephone number. She said she didn't have a telephone. (Eccentric!) Then I asked for her address, so that I could come by and see her. She gave me a post office box number in Los Angeles. I got the picture. She did not want us to see her in Los Angeles, and the man with the dogs was probably the reason.

Within a few years Anaïs became the darling of the lecture circuit and feminist circles. In 1974 she spoke at a symposium at the Palace of Fine Arts in San Francisco dedicated to a celebration of Woman. I took four of my five children to the event. Two of them were young adults and two were early teenagers, and they were all thrilled to see their famous aunt. After the program was over we went up to her and I introduced my children to her. "Oh!" she said to my daughter, Lisa, "I'm so glad to see you at last. You were always asleep when I came." (She never set foot inside my house. Maybe she was thinking of somebody else, or maybe she said that to all young people.) My handsome thirteen-year-old son, Eric, asked if he could kiss her, and of course she said yes. That was the last time I saw Aunt Anaïs.

Soon after that 1974 visit she became ill with cancer. She was too ill to travel back and forth between Los Angeles and New York, and so she stayed in Los Angeles. Eventually she let Uncle Joaquín know her address, and he went down to visit her. He gave me her address, and I wrote to her in 1975 or 1976. She responded with a warm letter, expressing regret that she never got to know me or to see me over the years after I became an adult. She died early in 1977.

LILA ROSENBLUM

Anaïs was the dearest friend I had for nearly twenty years, from 1946 until 1963, when we lost geographic but never emotional contact. That, in spite of the fear she expressed that her need to split her time between Ian Hugo in New York and Rupert Pole in California (what she referred to as her "divided life") would prevent her from being the kind of friend she wanted to be.

Our friendship began in the fall of 1946, just after the release of *Ladders to Fire*, the first of her books to be published commercially in the United States. That time and occasion are engraved permanently in my memory, when so much else has faded after nearly fifty years, because I was so proud of having engineered the meeting.

As a twenty-one-year-old New York University liberal arts student with literary aspirations, I was working part-time at Lawrence R. Maxwell Books at 45 Christopher Street in Greenwich Village. The banner hanging outside the shop, like something from a British tavern, read "At the Sign of the Dancing Bear," referring to the way my boss, Larry Maxwell, liked to think of himself — as a big, cuddly, dancing bear. And it was to that side of him I'd appealed when I convinced him to throw a party for Anaïs after learning that *Ladders* was about to be published by E. P. Dutton.

I had been longing to find a way to meet her for some time — ever since I'd first come upon her name a year or two before in a secondhand bookstore, whose name I can't remember. Though the store no longer exists, I can still see it clearly in my mind's eye

— planted firmly between Jones and Cornelia Streets on the south side of West Fourth.

There I found Henry Miller's *The Cosmological Eye,* which includes two essays about Anaïs reprinted from European publications. "Une Etre Etoilique" (or "A Starry Being") refers to her as-yet-unpublished diaries as "a great pageant of the times patiently and humbly delineated by one who considered herself as nothing, by one who had almost completely effaced herself in the effort to arrive at a true understanding of life."[1] I was fascinated.

The other essay, "Scenario (A Film with Sound)," based on *House of Incest,* haunted me and drove me to search everywhere for the first edition of that book (published in Paris under the Siana Editions imprint in 1936) and for anything else of hers. That included *D. H. Lawrence: An Unprofessional Study* (published in Paris by Edward W. Titus in 1932) and the books (*Winter of Artifice, Under a Glass Bell,* and *This Hunger*) she had printed in this country herself.

When I finally found *House of Incest,* I fell in love with its tantalizing suggestiveness and the poetry of the writing — like nothing I had ever encountered. I was astounded and captivated.

That's why the news in *Publishers' Weekly* that Dutton was bringing out *Ladders to Fire* struck me hard. Here was the opportunity I'd been waiting for! If only I could figure out a way to convince Old Trotskyite Larry to throw a party for her.

To this day, I'm not sure how I managed it — I, a little pipsqueak from Youngstown, Ohio — just a part-time clerk in his store. He couldn't have cared less about Anaïs or her work, it turned out later. But his "front" was so good that I'm not sure she ever knew. Because, of course, he played up to her that night and thereafter, wanting to absorb some of the fame we all saw coming.

His way of showing it bothered her. As she writes in her *Diary,* "I had never met anyone before who made me feel from the beginning that I was a celebrity and that whatever I did would become the subject of an anecdote. It was distressing. It was artificial."[2]

But as I think back on that night from the distance of nearly half a century, not only Larry was artificial. For me, the whole evening had an air of artifice. Intoxicating artifice.

Standing way in the back of the store — all excited in my best

7

party clothes — with a crowd of already tipsy people in a haze of cigarette smoke between me and the entrance, I watched her lead an entourage through the door. She seemed to me to sweep in, followed by Eugene Walter and a train of young men.

Eugene (if I remember correctly) was the son of the famous conductor Bruno Walter, and was later to make a name for himself by writing one of the first critical books about Hollywood films. But that night, Eugene was not famous. His only claim to fame then, so far as I know, was the Hat . . . the headpiece . . . the headgear she was wearing. He'd designed it for her. "A paper crown" she calls it in her *Diary.*[3]

But to me, that description hardly does it justice. The topper I remember was a tower of translucent cellophane, sutured and braided and twisted and knotted and woven into a magnificent headdress that glistened multicolored in the light as she glided slowly toward me.

I stood there, transfixed.

How I managed to introduce myself I can't imagine. But I must have said something. I'm sure we must have talked, briefly. But whatever words passed between us I can no longer conjure up.

All I know now is that a week or so later she telephoned me at home, where I was sick in bed, and asked to visit. I can still hear her voice — high and somehow wispy with the thick French accent it never lost.

How did I react? I have no idea. But I guess I must have been surprised, delighted, and apprehensive. She was my idol and more than twenty years older. What could she possibly see in me?

Little did I — or she, for that matter — know then how much we already had in common. Not only literary interests, but also Gonzalo.

Gonzalo Moré was a man who had been her lover after Miller. In 1936, they lived together in a houseboat on the Seine. But even more to the point, so far as I was concerned, he was presently her partner in the Gemor (*Gonzalo More*) Press, the press she'd set up in 1941 to print her books after repeated unsuccessful attempts to interest commercial publishers.

But I knew nothing about their connection in 1946, when she came to visit me. Nor had she any idea that I even knew him, let alone that I might be the young friend he'd been wanting her to meet.

How could she have, when he'd been such an unlikely person for me to know? He was a bronzed, six-foot Peruvian Indian who two years earlier had met me at a bar, and I was a nineteen-year-old who saw him as old enough (as he may have been) to be my father.

I still think of him as the handsomest man I've ever seen. He may also have been the most thoughtful. Every night when the bar closed, he made a point of walking me home without ever asking for so much as a goodnight kiss. That was rare enough in those wartime days for me to appreciate and remember.

The Sevilla, a bar and restaurant where Gonzalo and I met in 1944 and continued to meet every night for at least a year, maybe more, was across the street from the building in which I'd shared an apartment with college roommates the second semester I spent in New York. Today, the Sevilla still stands on the corner of West Fourth and Charles Streets.

Though I was an inveterate people-watcher and Gonzalo had been a regular there for years, I don't think I noticed him at first. But eventually, I couldn't help singling him out, because his looks and attire were so unusual: a tall man with red-bronze skin, sculptured features, and greying hair wearing a bright velvet tunic over corduroy pants. How different he looked from the other men at the bar, dressed (as they were for the most part) in fatigues or uniforms — drinking, smoking, and talking animatedly with one another or with young women in peasant skirts and ballet slippers.

After I don't know how many days (and drinks), I grew brave enough to speak up in support of whatever I heard him say, whether about the war or about domestic news. And that may have been what made him begin to notice me. In any case, we became friends.

That didn't mean I knew anything about his life. None of us knew what the others did during the day, and Gonzalo was the most mysterious (certainly to me and perhaps to everyone) of the Sevilla crowd. I didn't even know where he went when he left me each night or whom he saw before arriving at the bar.

By no stretch of the imagination could I possibly have dreamed

9

— sitting in the Sevilla or walking home with him after the bar closed at four in the morning — that the exotic woman friend he'd told me about again and again, the one he said he wanted me to meet, was my secret treasure, Anaïs. The possibility that she might actually be aware of my existence would have been hard for me to believe.

Yet, that is exactly what she told me some time after our friendship solidified, which had started to happen on that day she came to visit me in 1946. "When we finally met," she says in the *Diary*, "we talked like sisters, though Lila was much younger." She continues:

> Talking with her I am reminded of things I did not write about because they were too painful. Lila was crippled by an unusual illness. Half the time she was bedridden. But . . . her spirit is undefeated. . . . She worked, how I do not know. Her place was filled with books. We talked analysis and life.[4]

Oh, yes, we talked that day and for all the years we were close. We talked and talked and talked. We talked analysis and life and books and writing and gossip and lovers and cooking and dancing and New York and Los Angeles and Paris and more.

Each time I came away feeling understood and appreciated and loved, and light as air — to such an extent that a jealous friend of mine once remarked, "Anaïs says, 'Let there be light,' and there is light."

And there was. For her, too.

How did it happen that she and I — so different in so many ways — became such intimate friends and confidantes for so long?

For much of the two years after the 1946 visit, we were unable to see one another in person. My health had forced me to move out of New York. Though she was moving around a great deal during that period, none of her travels brought her to Arizona where I was living and attending the university. Still, we kept in touch by mail.

After those two years, however, my move to Los Angeles, not far from Pasadena, where she was living with Rupert in Sierra Madre, enabled us to get together on a regular basis. The first time I remember, she had come in tears to my apartment on El Tovar Place in West Hollywood.

That was also the first time I'd ever seen her upset. (She was being treated badly by Rupert's family.) Seeing my idol that way melted away the inequality between us forever. The fact that she had come to *me* for comfort and understanding changed everything for me — not only my feelings about her but also about myself.

From that point on, whenever we were together, she made me feel good about myself. I'm not sure how she did that, but I think she had a special gift for making someone — not only me — feel like the most important person in her world *at that particular moment*, whenever it happened to be.

She was also generous in sharing everything she had with me — from little things like jewelry to her daily swim in the neighbors' pool to big things like money and all of her friends. The one who became most important to me was James Leo Herlihy (later to become the well-known author of *Blue Denim* and *All Fall Down*).

Shortly after the time she came to me for comfort, she took me to the Satyr Bookshop on, I believe, Sunset Boulevard where he was working — especially to meet him. Jim was perched atop a high ladder, almost on the ceiling, eating raisins and almonds, his exclusive diet at the time. (I don't think I'll ever forget the sight.) That did it for me. We clicked instantly.

Here's what she wrote me about our friendship in 1951:

I can now thank you for doing a great deal for me. Your warmth, and your faith in me, and your insight helped me in one of those moments which occur frequently, when I lose my own world, my creative world, because of my human devotions. It was so when I was a girl, a woman and now: the human being came first, and was devoted, and the creation was put aside, sacrificed. As a human being taking care of others, I felt essential, as an artist less. It was the same when I was ready to destroy the *Diary* for the harm it might do, humanly.

So finding in you, as in Jim, friends for whom both were essential reawakened me, too — to work — to live also more extensively . . .

The current flows between you and Jim and me and I feel you will give each other what I would like to, but so seldom can because of the divided pattern of my life — draining my strength. Your fears buried you temporarily, mine keep me from landing or anchoring as I should.[5]

If not for Anaïs and the faith she had in me, I might have none of what I value today — more than forty years of sobriety, because she told me the truth about what drinking was doing to me; a successful psychotherapy practice, because she urged me to become an analyst; and a happy life, because by the example of our relationship she taught me how to love. I cherish her memory.

NOTES

1. Henry Miller, *The Cosmological Eye* (Norfolk, CT: New Directions, 1939), 278.
2. *The Diary of Anaïs Nin, 1947–1955,* ed. Gunther Stuhlmann (New York: Harcourt Brace Jovanovich, 1974), 237–38.
3. *The Diary of Anaïs Nin, 1944–1947,* ed. Gunther Stuhlmann (New York: Harcourt Brace Jovanovich, 1971), 163.
4. *The Diary of Anaïs Nin, 1947–1955,* 43.
5. Undated letter from Anaïs Nin to Lila Rosenblum.

WILLIAM BURFORD

I first met Anaïs Nin in 1946 or 1947 when I was a student at Amherst College. She had come to give a reading from her stories, a reading arranged by Kimon Friar, who was teaching that year at the college in the English department. Friar wanted to introduce the students to literature that they would not otherwise know from taking the traditional English courses. He had formed a little coterie with himself at the center and including as its bright star James Merrill, son of the founder of the brokerage firm bearing his name, who was a well-known Amherst alumnus. At the time no one on the Amherst campus knew that Friar and Merrill were lovers, though there was muted gossip among certain elements of the student body, for whom the two held an aloof disdain. Part of Friar's plan for a kind of literary liberation of the Amherst English students was to bring avant-garde figures from New York to the college. When the news was bruited that someone named Anaïs Nin was coming, there was very little excitement because almost no one had the least idea who she was or what she had written. These were the dark days of Anaïs's career.

Her reading was to take place in the Octagon, a lovely nineteenth-century building in the shape its name implies and that housed, appropriately, the music department. As for the Dickinson House, it was closed to visitors and to faculty and students as well. There was no sense on the campus or in the town of a rare muse's presence, named Emily, that once graced the place. If Kimon Friar had brought Anaïs from New York to Amherst as a kind of recollection of Emily Dickinson, of the muse come home again, then he had miscalculated. The English department took no part in receiving Anaïs at the college; the event went virtually unattended. It turned out that Kimon had also invited Djuna Barnes, lesbian author of *Nightwood,* one of his favorite books, whose principal character he identified with; but Djuna Barnes had refused to share the program with Anaïs and had not come. So much for the avant-garde at Amherst, at least in those days.

After Anaïs's reading, our small group went to a party at the house of a mathematics professor and his wife who were friends of Merrill and were a kind of island of good conversation and sympathetic listening for him and other students as well. The wife did not approve of Friar and thought him a bad influence on Jimmy, as she affectionately called Merrill, but had given way when he asked her to give the party. It was there, under these conditions, that I met Anaïs. Who is it who said, "The only real luxury is human relationships"? Frieda Lawrence. Anaïs had written about D. H. This brief observation of Frieda's speaks exactly for what happened when Anaïs and I met that evening, after the debacle of her appearance at Amherst. The few people who were there did not go to speak to her and she and I were left to ourselves. I cannot remember what the subject of our conversation was; nor did we engage in the kind of veiled, amorous play that takes place between a young man and an older woman, though our talk was, indeed, a kind of seduction. Nietzsche in *Thus Spake Zarathustra* tells how in the state of inspiration all the speech and language doors fly open before us. Our meeting was something like that. Though Anaïs was often accused of writing purple prose, my impression of her conversation, at least, both then and later, was that she was quite clear-headed. The evening at Amherst ended with Anaïs inviting me to come to New York to a soiree at her apartment in the Village. She also invited Jim Merrill. We were to stay at his mother's townhouse in the upper fifties. When the day came, as we were riding in the taxi to Anaïs's address, Merrill suddenly cautioned me, "Don't tell her a thing. She writes it all down." But the stir over these supposedly dangerous diaries seemed inconsequential to me. I did not wonder what was in them. Their chief function was to give Anaïs something of the aura of a Sybil, except that she did not burn her leaves or scatter them on the wind. Little did I realize that Anaïs's diary pages would have an interest for a large number of people. Nor at that time, when I first knew her, were prognostications for their success in evidence. When I mentioned Anaïs to Howard Moss, poetry editor of *The New Yorker,* he said to me, "I wouldn't touch Anaïs Nin with a ten-foot pole." But there was another diary besides her own that had attracted a number of people in Anaïs's circle, and this was the *Diary* of the Russian dancer Vaslav Nijinsky. Henry Miller tells us in his *First Impressions of Greece* that in 1939 at the invitation of Lawrence Durrell he joined Durrell on the island of Corfu where Durrell was then living, and found in Durrell's library there the *Diary* of Nijinsky. Reading it, Miller at once chose it as one of the very few texts he would reread throughout his life.[1] As he says in *The Colossus of Maroussi,* "I also reread Nijinsky's *Diary.* I know I shall read it again and again. There are only a few books which I can read over and over."[2] Almost certainly it was through Henry Miller that Anaïs knew of this *Diary.*

She asked me one day a bit cryptically, "Do you keep a diary?" I did not feel a connection between her question and any necessity of mine. That recognition would come later. For the moment we were in the midst of a day of blowing snow, seen through the window of her apartment, and we felt the need to be out in it, to take a walk in the Village. After a while we stopped in front of a bookshop window, and there on the other side of the glass, half obscured by the heavy snowfall, was the book, opened to the title page:

THE DIARY OF
VASLAV NIJINSKY
Edited by
ROMOLA NIJINSKY
LONDON
VICTOR GOLLANCZ LTD
1937

I did not know then that it had first been published the year before in New York, but such bibliographic facts were not the point of our finding the book in that snowy window. Anaïs excitedly advised me to buy it. "Bill, you must have it. It is one of *your* books, that you must know." When I hesitated, reminded by the thickening storm that I had to drive back to Amherst and might need money to buy gas on the road, still she urged me to take the book. "You can't leave it behind." So, of course, I didn't. I took Nijinsky and his *Diary* back to Amherst with me, wrapped in a newspaper and bound with twine against the storm, a bit like swaddling clothes, a thick packet I could feel under my arm, against my rib cage, Dionysos born from Zeus's thigh. I reached my car parked near Anaïs's apartment and bid her goodbye, thanking her for the book which, though I had bought it, seemed more a gift from her.

It was almost a year, however, before I read Nijinsky's *Diary*, a year in which Anaïs and I grew more distant, so that we never, as I recall, discussed that astonishing document or her reasons for wanting me to be aware of it. Henry Miller in *First Impressions of Greece* had said, "It is important to know about Nijinsky."[3] Why is it? Miller does not entirely tell us. A part of the reason is that Nijinsky had triumphed — and the word is Miller's — over his homosexuality. Certainly the story of Nijinsky's sexual life is one of the most instructive of such stories. But also and more significantly, his *Diary* shows what happens to a basic human faculty, language, when it is breaking down. Nijinsky's *Diary*, after we feel the pain of his self-exposure, his psychological nakedness, is filled with startling word outbursts asserting his determination to speak, to be heard. He cries out: I want to say, say.[4] But this is the very skill he does not have, except by fits and starts. After reading the *Diary* I wondered what Anaïs would have said about this language catastrophe, as it were, she who could write almost ceaselessly, with unflagging ease over the years. But Anaïs and I had grown apart by the time I read Nijinsky's *Diary*, and in any case she did not like problems. Rather, she wanted to live constantly in the non-problematic, the dream, as she called it. Her first letter to me had begun with, "When I lie down to dream. . . ."

I saw Anaïs last, or rather her ghost, her small white face, in the crowd at Nureyev's funeral. We joined hands and skipped a little dance, she in her famous black dress, through the streets of

Paris. All problems shed. Though Nureyev's ravaged face and
Nijinsky's blank one were there also. They joined her in saying

> Do not surrender to sadness
> Do not surrender to sadness[5]

NOTES

1. Henry Miller, *First Impressions of Greece* (Santa Barbara:
   Capra, 1973), 35–36.
2. Henry Miller, *The Colossus of Maroussi* (New York: New Directions, 1958), 22.
3. Miller, *First Impressions of Greece*, 35.
4. Vaslav Nijinsky, *The Diary of Vaslav Nijinsky*, ed. Romola
   Nijinsky (London: Victor Gollancz, 1937), 89.
5. Quotation from Jalāl al-Dīn Rūmī; source unknown.

ANATOLE BROYARD

Sheri [Donatti] took me to see Anaïs Nin, who lived in the Village at that time.[1] According to her diary, which was published years later, Anaïs had spiritually adopted Sheri, describing her as the ghost of her own younger self. She spoke of Sheri as a disciple. "So they come," she wrote, "out of the stories, out of the novels, magnetized by affinities, by similar characters."[2] Sheri was an "orphaned child of poverty . . . pleading, hurt, vulnerable, breathless."[3] "She talks as I write, as if I had created a language for her feelings."[4]

Anaïs's apartment was a top-floor walk-up on Thirteenth Street. Everyone Sheri knew lived on top floors, probably because it was cheaper, but I thought of them as struggling to get to the light. Besides Anaïs and her husband, Ian Hugo, a pleasant, self-effacing man, there was a young couple whose names I no longer remember. The young man held a guitar across his knees, but you could see that he would never play it, that it was just part of a composition, like the guitars in Cubist paintings.

Though I hadn't yet read anything by Anaïs, I'd heard of her. It was said that she and Henry Miller had once lived on a houseboat on the Seine. Later I would learn that she had attracted Otto Rank, who allegedly trained her as a psychoanalyst, and who asked her to rewrite his almost unreadable books. In New York she had an odd acquaintance with Edmund Wilson. After Mary McCarthy left him, he developed a crush on Anaïs and took her to his apartment, which Mary had stripped of furniture. When he

18

reviewed one of her novels, you could see him struggling between his desire and his taste. As usual, though, she had the last word in her diary. Summarizing their evening together, she said, "He wanted me to help him reconstruct his life, to help him choose a couch. . . . But I wanted to leave."[5]

Anaïs was a medium-sized woman with a very pale face, like a Japanese actress. She was classical-looking, in the sense of a form that has become rigidified. Her hair was dark, straight, parted in the middle and pulled back. Her lipstick was precise, her eyebrows shaved off and penciled in, giving the impression that she had written her own face. Her figure was trim but without elasticity, its movements willed and staccato. She was pretty in the way of women in old black-and-white movies. There was a suggestion of the vamp about her, and, in fact, she was later to become a kind of Theda Bara of modern literature.

It was impossible to guess her age. Her teeth looked false and her face had the arbitrary smoothness of one that had been lifted, but I thought this unlikely. It was possible she lifted it herself by the sheer force of her will.

Yet she was impressive in her way, an evocative figure. She reminded me of the melancholy Paris hotels of expatriate writing and I could imagine her, wearing an ambiguous fur, sitting defiantly, or insouciantly, in a café. While I could not imagine her in bed with Henry Miller, that may have been his fault.

There was an aura about her, a sense that she was holding a séance. The atmosphere was charged with her energy. When she gave me her hand and looked searchingly into my eyes, I could feel her projecting an image of herself, one that was part French, part flamenco, part ineffable. When she said, You are Anatole, I immediately became Anatole in a way I hadn't been before.

As I listened to her talk — for it was understood that she did most of the talking, even if it was to ask us questions — it occurred to me that she and Sheri deformed their speech as Chinese women used to deform their feet. Her talk was pretty much like the things she wrote in her diaries. An entry from this time gives a good idea of what she sounded like: "Think of the ballet exercises. The hand reproduces resistance to water. And what is painting but absolute transparency? It is art which is ecstasy, which is

Paradise, and water."[6] Here's another: "It is possible I never learned the names of birds in order to discover the bird of peace, the bird of paradise, the bird of the soul, the bird of desire."[7] Her conversation flirted with all the arts and settled on none, like someone who doesn't really want to buy a book browsing in a bookshop. I was careful about what I said, because I could see that Anaïs was important to Sheri. I was afraid of coming out with something literal-minded, like, Were you bothered by rats when you lived on the houseboat?

Though Anaïs described Sheri in her *Diary* as "a figure out of the past,"[8] I thought that Sheri was a later, not an earlier, version. Anaïs was already out of style, and Sheri was just coming in. Anaïs was like someone at a party, dancing, drinking, and batting her eyes, and Sheri was the morning after the party. Anaïs was unconscious of the picture she made, and Sheri was all consciousness. While Sheri was always listening to herself, always rehearsing and revising, Anaïs had already posed for her statue. She had posed for it without knowing where it would be put up.

Sheri too was watching herself more than she usually did, if that was possible, perhaps because she felt the pull of Anaïs, the temptation to be "magnetized by affinities."[9] With all this doublethinking, with no one simply speaking up, the conversation grew so stilted that Anaïs was forced to bring out a bottle of wine. With a sudden swoop, she deposited the bottle in my hands, together with an old-fashioned corkscrew. The look she gave me made it clear that this was to be a test of sorts — but of what?

I had no choice but to accept the challenge. In what I hoped was a confident, heterosexual manner, I applied myself firmly, but with an ironic awareness, to drawing the cork. When the screw was all the way in, I pulled slowly and steadily on the handle. I did all the usual things, and I did them in slow motion, so it came as a rude shock to me when the handle broke off.

It simply came away in my hand. I was holding the bottle with the screw in one hand and the wooden stump in the other. My first thought was, It's not my fault. I did it right. She can't blame me. Then I tried to fit the handle back on while Anaïs leaned forward and watched me. Was it a trick? I wondered. A surrealist or dadaist joke? She was smiling, as if I had confirmed her intuition about me. I knew that whatever I did, I would confirm her intuition.

I wanted to fling the bottle against the wall, but she was already pressing another corkscrew into my hand, an identical one. I didn't want it, but I didn't see any way of refusing. I gave the thing a little preliminary twist in the air, just to see whether it would hold together. The original screw was still in place and with some trouble I managed to get it out. Then I worked the new one in, even more deliberate now. It took me five minutes to get it all the way in. I turned it evenly, so as not to put any unnecessary stress on the handle.

I pulled very gradually, gently at first, then more strongly. Nothing happened. The cork didn't budge. I couldn't imagine why not — it wasn't as if this was an ancient bottle of wine that had been sealed by time itself. To get a better purchase, I put the bottle on the floor between my feet.

What came next still seems incredible to me. Sometimes I think it didn't actually happen, that my memory is playing tricks. But it did happen: Before my eyes, I saw the corkscrew slowly emerge from the cork. It didn't break off; the cork didn't crumble. The screw simply straightened out, so that I was holding in my hand something that resembled an ice pick.

I felt like a person in a dream. I shook myself, tried to collect my wits, to stop the blush that was rising to my face. What should I have done? What would Henry Miller have done in my place? Otto Rank? Edmund Wilson?

Anaïs took the bottle and the corkscrew and put them on a table. Perhaps she had never meant for it to be opened. She turned and looked at me through narrowed eyes. I can see, she said, that you are a most interesting young man.

In her *Diary*, there was nothing about the corkscrews, but I was described as "handsome, sensual, ironic."[10] I wasn't fooled: All the young men in her *Diary* were handsome, sensual, and ironic.

NOTES

1. Anaïs Nin refers to Sheri Donatti as Sherry Martinelli in *The*

Diary of Anaïs Nin, 1944–1947, ed. Gunther Stuhlmann (New York: Harcourt Brace Jovanovich, 1971), 108, 132, 231. The author of the poem "Goodbye Anaïs" signs herself Sheri Martinelli in *Anaïs: An International Journal* 12 (1994): 77. Deirdre Bair refers to her as Sherry Donati in *Anaïs Nin: A Biography* (New York: Putnam's, 1995), 328, 627. The events Broyard describes occurred in 1947.

2. Nin, *Diary,* 107.
3. Ibid., 107–8.
4. Ibid., 108.
5. Ibid., 83.
6. Ibid., 8.
7. Ibid., 55.
8. Ibid., 107.
9. Ibid.
10. Ibid., 180.

HARRIET ZINNES

If, as Paul Muldoon has the subject of his poem "Incantata" suggest, life is fated, a "done deal," friendship itself would have nothing random about it. Its occurrence would be inexorably prearranged. Yet when I consider my friendship with Anaïs Nin, there was nothing fated about it. It was certainly by chance that we met. I was not living in New York City, though not too far away. I was living with my family in Princeton where my husband was teaching physics at the university and I, having two small children, was teaching part-time at Rutgers. Because of my domestic duties, I rarely visited New York. It was in 1961, when we were beginning our Princeton years, that the poet Daisy Aldan — we had been friends since college — suggested that I review *Seduction of the Minotaur*. I did review the book. The review led to an enduring friendship. It is interesting that later it was Nin who in her turn suggested I review Marianne Hauser's *Prince Ishmael*. That too led to a long friendship.

In the late fifties we had been living in Norman, Oklahoma, where my children were born and where my husband had his first teaching job. When he was invited to Princeton, though there were many aspects of Oklahoma that we both considered fascinating, he accepted, not only of course because of the exciting physics department but also because he was pleased at the possibility of living in the East again. But for me a return to the East was filled with all kinds of anxieties. As a mother I worried about life in the unprotected East and as a poet I worried about my return to the literary and art "scene." It was gratifying to have Daisy ease my way back into that ominous literary world that would become one of the subjects of my long correspondence with Anaïs Nin. It was Daisy, too, whom Anaïs herself frequently relied on in her early period in New York for the coordination of literary matters. As I reread Anaïs's letters to me in connection with the writing of this article, I was pleased to see how often Daisy's name appears as a kind of symbol of one who considered work rather than "making it" as the true goal of the writer. "Being published or not," Anaïs would frequently write to me in one way or another, "has no relation to your quality." Or she might say that the literary world was "toxic," filled with "poison," and that all prizes were "meaningless" and political, even the Nobel Prize. Therefore, the "essential thing" for a writer "is the work," and especially for the poet, because "poetry is a pure and detached noncommercial thing at best."

But of course all this urging on the part of Anaïs on my return to New York to forget publication, reviews, invitations for readings, lectures, and so on, and to concentrate only on producing the poems and stories, was a bit ironic. I remember her insistence on this point at our first lunch at her Greenwich Village apartment (so sparse, without any paintings, with only the large blowups of scenes from her husband Ian Hugo's films). Nin was never one to forget her enormous need for recognition. Even in later years with her fame certainly established beyond the acclaim of the early Bohemia and avant-garde, she was constantly at work to hold on to that fame — even as she simultaneously worked hard on her fiction and diaries. "I work as few writers do," she had once written to me. But she also at the same time was hard at work on her correspondence. "No one understands," she complained to me in the early 1970s, "that mail has become one of my heaviest burdens." Part of the reason for what can be called her publicity industry (it was that energetic) through correspondence and other means was Nin's dismay at the frequent criticism (especially, she felt, by men) of her fiction. Subsequent criticism of the *Diary* was similar but of a more subdued nature since many critics saw the *Diary* as historically important for its bold psychological revelations, its interpretation of unrepressed twentieth-century egos.

The attacks on the fiction were more unrestrained because of what was seen as slight, weakly and sentimentally lyrical, without the necessary strength of action and hard plot, with characters hardly distinguishable from the superficially "poetic" author. There is no doubt that Nin had a more receptive audience in Europe, especially in France. When, therefore, my family went to live in Geneva, Switzerland, where my husband was invited to do research at the university (later I was given the position of Visiting Professor of American Literature), Anaïs felt that the rich European experience I would be having would change and deepen (perhaps Europeanize?) my poetry. As a matter of fact, it was in Geneva that I discovered Jacques Prévert and began translating him for a book that would later become the bilingual edition *Blood and Feathers*. Anaïs was sure that living in Europe would lead to changes. She quoted Lawrence to me, Lawrence, who was the subject of her first and to this writer one of her best books, to the effect that I must experience, taste, and see, and to Nin such tasting was most effectively (and deliciously) experienced in Europe, particularly if one became acquainted with its artists and poets. In Europe, she claimed, one could more easily experience what is rich and deep, especially what is sensuous and unrepressed, because in materialistic America even the writer was not free. America to Nin was all competition, marketing; it was openly hostile toward the arts. In the pre-Vietnam War years, Nin sensed that America was "an angry country." She anticipated an explosion. Despite her years in the States and her real joy in living in California, Nin always yearned for the Europe that was still tantalizing her.

Her years in Paris and in Louveciennes with her husband Ian Hugo (and fitfully with Henry Miller) were chaotic and fraught with conflicts, guilt, and illusion. Some of these feelings were portrayed in the film *Henry and June* despite its depiction of an awakening of sexuality in the character of Anaïs, who in the film seemed more like an unsophisticated schoolgirl fascinated by the assumed dregs of Bohemia than the real Anaïs, that is, the significant writer she was becoming. But Paris was always in the writer's mind the key to her work and life. When important European critics received her work with enthusiasm, this only confirmed her feelings. She wrote to me on December 13, 1969, about her critical acceptance in Paris: "I felt completely accepted by the best critics as I never felt in USA except by the special people, like you." (Perhaps I should exclude the last phrase — a reader must remember that she was writing to me!)

Because Anaïs and I rarely lived in the same place, our meetings were not frequent. At times we both were so busy that a meeting would be impossible even if we happened to be in the same city. In the later years of her life she traveled often. She was able to describe, for example, in a letter to me dated August 16, 1969, how her "trip to Morocco was a break in intensity of work and correspondence — a fabulous country. Greece dull, after Cambodia and Japan — Turkey dull too," and her words about America were becoming characteristic: "The weeks of escape from the violent US scene was [*sic*] healing though." Frequently letters were written on a plane — I remember how when she was on a flight on Japan Airlines how happy she was with the beauty and service that anticipated what she saw later everywhere in the country itself. Anaïs might be visiting in New York while I was there but one of us would find it impossible to find a convenient time. When I was living in Geneva, for example, Anaïs did happen to visit the city but again we could not meet because she was there for so limited a time, with so many professional engagements, that it was impossible. I never visited Los Angeles while Anaïs lived there. We spoke over the phone, of course. It is my great regret and sorrow that during her final illness I was not able to visit her. I remember how at one time nearing the end I could only speak to her companion Rupert Pole, whom I had met some years earlier. During that illness, Anaïs's letters were never filled with self-pity. On July 11, 1975, she was still giving me addresses of magazines and editors to whom I should send new work and asking me how my work was going, how my mood was, even though, without soliciting pity, she wrote that she had experienced a "six-month fight against cancer, three months in the hospital, surgery, and chemotherapy with all its side effects. . . ." This is a woman to whom dedication to the word was central but dedication to "US" (as she sometimes referred to her "circle" of friends) came a very close second. Was it because of so many early negative reactions to Anaïs's work that she yearned, as she wrote to me once, "of being loved, accepted by *everybody*"? Yet even when her work was being accepted she seemed to cling to the idea of a kind of universal rejection. There was therefore a degree of exaggeration in her emotional response to criticism. She was praised and known early on by the American avant-garde, as I have already indicated, but of course she wanted acceptance by the prestigious critics. It was indeed the critic Edmund Wilson, with whom Anaïs had had a short affair, who had helped to make her work known to a larger public. I remember, however, walking in the Village while I was still in college, stopping at a bookshop window, looking at what probably were the very books Nin herself had hand set, and thinking how wonderful it would be to meet such a writer. Such a meeting was inconceivable to a young undergraduate — just because Anaïs Nin then already seemed to be an established writer.

Friendship sometimes had a difficult time when the friend was a critic of the writer's work too. Or sometimes Anaïs, whose sustenance was friendship, lamented the fact of "missed" friendships — as she wrote to me early in our own friendship: "so many missed friendships which don't bloom. I think of that while writing about those which happen." She was then thinking of the time she wrote a fan letter to the poet Jean Garrigue, whom she later met but with whom she never developed a friendship.

But there was, as I suggested, the difficulty that arose if a friend was even the least bit critical in a published critique of the writer's work. In my review of *House of Incest*, I treated it as a novel and, like others, I'm afraid, criticized it for its lack of action and plot. She was very upset though she quoted Gide, who said that we must let others interpret work. She rejected my analysis because she felt that I was expecting from a prose poem what I had a right to demand from a novel. But perhaps what was more significant in her plea for my understanding of the work, in the light of the revelations in the recently published "unexpurgated" *Diary* of 1932-34, was her description of what she said was the theme of *House of Incest*. She wrote that the "book's theme is not so much incest as Jung's theory that most of our first loves take place within the family and are (symbolically) incestuous — a closed world."

There were at least two public occasions that were important in the development of our friendship. One was the remarkable turnout against the Vietnam War at Queens College of the City of New York that I had organized at the suggestion of the poets Galway Kinnell and Robert Bly. The students were magnificent in their attention and enthusiasm as the poets and other writers read their work and spoke against the war. Strange that I can't remember the names of the other celebrated writers who joined the protest. Anaïs was splendid in her quiet elegant way — her always slightly foreign sounds that gave to her words a kind of pure musicality.

The other occasion was all her own. I had invited Anaïs to give a talk to the students. Again, the audience was large and attentive. It was the beginning of the women's movement, so that the women students experienced special joy in hearing Anaïs, then an extremely celebrated writer, explain that above all it was necessary to move from "the dream outward" in order to perfect and complete the total woman, even as her external and quotidian world includes the complementary world of men. On April 15, 1971, in anticipation of Nin's visit, I sent to the English department staff for them to read to their students the following announcement — as I read it now, almost twenty-five years later, unforgivably hyperbolic, and perhaps aesthetically naive:

It is interesting that within a week we are having as visitors here at Queens College two writers to whom the world of the dream has been the living source of their creative work. The poet Robert Bly is of course very different from the novelist and diarist Anaïs Nin. But both have taken what seems to be the only way for the writer to survive in a world where, as Bly would probably have it, the Gross National Product is more important than the life of the imagination — or what Miss Nin might call the exploration of the unconscious, that "universal ocean in which all of us have roots." The collection of Miss Nin's novels called significantly *Cities of the Interior* goes to these roots, and the stories emerge, as she says, "from the dream outward."

As long ago as 1932 when Miss Nin was a very young woman she wrote what she called *An Unprofessional Study of D. H. Lawrence.* To this day it is the most important PROFES-

SIONAL study of the writer who like Miss Nin felt abstraction an anathema and the senses, the living experience and the dream the vital source. Even at the time of the Lawrence book Miss Nin's diaries had made her very name magical in international art and literary circles though the diaries still lay in ms and were seen by few. Today three of these diaries have been published and a fourth comes out next year — but there are still over 150 ms volumes ready to be edited and to be published. No longer is Miss Nin an underground figure — her works are no longer hand set but are published by commercial presses and receive lead reviews in the *New York Times Book Review*. But the magic and mystery still remain despite her published diaries. Perhaps it is that when beauty emerges in an original and powerful writer such as Anaïs Nin it becomes too mysterious to fathom, too mysterious to believe real. But Anaïs Nin is very real — the most real person I have ever had the pleasure to know.

Although a third public occasion did not occur, it almost did, and it involved Anaïs's husband Ian Hugo, the filmmaker, rather than the diarist herself. I tried to get a showing of his films at the college but because of lack of funds and the usual bureaucratic rules, it was impossible. But I remember how anxious Anaïs had been when in the mid-1960s Hugo was having trouble with his vision because of cataracts that were removed with surgery. She was also very proud (I cite this to underscore Anaïs's real and deep affection for Hugo) that Hugo made "his most beautiful film with only one eye."

There is so much more to say about a friendship that was indeed never feigning, that was always sympathetic, even to the extent at one point when I was having personal difficulties for Anaïs to suggest I see her own therapist, Dr. Inge Bogner. She was always very enthusiastic about therapy (of course she had become a therapist herself, and infamously, had slept with some famous ones). She wrote to me as evidence of her success with Dr. Bogner that it helped enormously to discuss with her therapist the shock she experienced when she received hostile reviews.

I'd like to end with something sentimental and sweet. My granddaughter, at this writing five years old — and almost as well traveled as the mature Anaïs because of her Harvard economist father — is named after Anaïs. Little Anaïs, who will be wearing when she is older, a scarf beloved by Anaïs that Rupert gave me as a remembrance, became the diarist's namesake because her mother, Angela, of French-Spanish-Indian ancestry, and a therapist, rejoices in a writer who, like herself, urges us all to go "from the dream outward."

DEENA METZGER

I met Anaïs Nin in Los Angeles in 1965. My then-husband, Reed Metzger, and I were invited to hear a string quartet play at the home of Abe and Leona Weiss. Seated next to me on a couch was a beautiful woman writing in a small book as the music played. I do not think she said a single word that evening. Afterwards, Leona asked me if I knew who she was. I didn't. She gave me *Cities of the Interior.* I hadn't known it was permitted to speak of the cities in the interior. I hadn't known it was possible to write the inner world in its own languages. I had been waiting for such a revelation. As I read the book, a road toward my own work opened.

I invited Anaïs and Rupert Pole to go sailing with Reed and me. We came back to the harbor at sunset. Darkness came on quickly, but in colors of magenta and orange. Anaïs disappeared for a long time; I thought she might not reappear. I was beginning to think about the borders between worlds, and it seemed to me that if anyone could travel back and forth across them, it was she. Almost thirty years later, I still write about such border crossings. Now, my work is informed by physics and astronomy, by a variety of spiritual teachings, by my own experiences and understanding, but then I was a young woman and what I needed to begin was the authorization Anaïs offered by asserting the fundamental reality of the dream.

Collages had recently been published. As I was drama and arts editor for the *Los Angeles Free Press,* I reviewed it. The last story in the book winds into the first story as a uroborus might find its

31

tail. Again, I was taken by the modification of linear time and space. A world that I recognized appeared like a phantom growing its rightful body.

That was the beginning of our friendship, which lasted until she died, and afterwards.

For many people, Anaïs is an enigma. For me, it has always been the opposite: she made the enigmatic meaningful. This was the basis of our friendship; together we explored the territories of the imagination.

When someone is a public figure, and when that someone dies, a set of questions constellates around her. Inevitably because of the nature of projection, different people inspire different inquiries. Over the years, I have been persistently asked to enumerate Anaïs's flaws or to address the question of narcissism. The question with which I would parry is: How responsible is a public figure for the needs of the people who gather around her, intrigued or sustained by her work and her life?

I prefer not to answer this question, either, because it is complex and in Anaïs's case would require a lengthy examination of the times in which she lived, attitudes toward women, the beginning of the women's movement, and also the cult of the male artist as hero or hero manqué to which she, like so many others, including those male artists themselves, fell victim and against which she rebelled. But I would like to tell two stories.

The first concerns a time when I came into her house and saw that she was deeply upset. "I am not a paragon," she cried out. "I will not be set upon a pedestal." It was one of the first times that I perceived her loneliness, and that moment confirmed my insistence on having a friendship with the person rather than the literary figure. The real woman was, of course, extraordinary — her writing did not come out of the air. She was remarkably intelligent and concerned with the nature of beauty as a powerful force in transforming life. To this idea, she was devoted, and she attempted in all the ways she knew to create a life that accorded with her beliefs or hopes. Also, her work mattered to her. She did not distinguish herself from it. We can say, then, that she had integrity. And like every other person of integrity, she triumphed and failed, she suffered and was joyous, she was absurd and magnificent.

The second event occurred just before the first *Diary* was published. She told me with some alarm that she had dreamed that she opened the door of her house and was overwhelmed by a blast of atomic radiation. She knew then that she was about to enter the ordeal of the public world and she did not know if she would survive it.

I am, like Anaïs, an essentially shy person but also deeply committed to the public world. My writing began with an investigation of the inner and the personal, and I was initiated into the domain of the diary or journal by her. Sometimes I am like two or more people in one body, and I know that she experienced similar dilemmas and divisions. She thought that it was necessary to bring the investigations and explorations in the diary out into the public world in part to heal the insidious schism between inner and outer which leads, most often, to the suppression or denigration of the intimate. But she also knew the cost.

As we know, Anaïs divided her time between Los Angeles and New York. It was a clever and difficult solution to a multi-valenced life. I saw her every time she was in Los Angeles, and in-between we sometimes had letters or postcards or calls. Over twelve years, we developed a routine that satisfied us. Anaïs wrote in the morning. I came over at noon and stayed until Rupert returned from work in the late afternoon. Sometimes we met in the evening at a party or for music or a literary event. The latter social events were not the core of our friendship but the more formal rituals through which relationships are often maintained.

I was with Anaïs on many important occasions: I was at her house one moment when she learned that Ian Hugo was seriously ill and another time when she discovered she had been betrayed. I accompanied her when she and Henry Miller returned their letters to each other. At one extreme, I gave a wild costume party to celebrate the publication of the first *Diary;* on the other, I decorated the hospital room when she was ill with cancer, trying to transform it into carnival. We celebrated and grieved together, shared the wonder and sorrow of the second wave of feminism, the contemplation of the reality and possibilities of woman's culture, and the range of anguish and joy, suffering and gratitude that composed our lives. Over the years we wrestled as writers and diarists with the essential issues of what should be said, could be said, must be said, what must be protected, what might be transformed, respecting the different needs of and responsibilities to self, other, and audience. But whatever the occasion, it was always a great pleasure to be with her because I learned so much from the interaction; I was sustained by the nature of our exchange, deeply encouraged as an artist and invariably nurtured by her passion to understand and her indomitable generosity.

For its anecdotal value, I like to tell the story of the meeting between Anaïs and Carlos Castañeda. My friend, the late anthropologist Barbara Myerhoff, had been in graduate school with Carlos. He had written what became *The Teachings of Don Juan* as his Ph.D. thesis and was concerned about making it public. He was not certain if it was white magic or black magic. He did not know what effect it would have in the world, and he did not want to do harm. Barbara wrested the manuscript from him and after reading it convinced him of its value before he destroyed it. Finally, he submitted the manuscript to the University of California Press, where it was seemingly ignored for a long time. Needless to say, none of us had the foresight to imagine how this book would be received in the world. But I knew that Anaïs was so enthusiastic a supporter of new writers and creativity that she almost never went to New York without someone's manuscript or project in hand; she devoted a good portion of her time and energy to battling the dominant commerical values and literary establishment in order to promote the work she believed in. She knew what it meant to be an "underground" writer and she was, until her death, indefatigable in her championship of fresh and original voices, men and women. And so I asked her to meet this young anthropologist and read the manuscript Barbara thought should definitely be published. The four of us had a lovely lunch at Anaïs's house. The Carlos who appeared, dressed quite formally in a gray suit and tie, was reserved and modest, and the conversation ambled from the difficulties of verifying and maintaining distinct epistemologies and of validating different ways of seeing, from extraordinary (at least by Western standards) reality to the exigencies of publishing. Anaïs read the manuscript, was impressed by it, and took it to New York. This was apparently the encouragement or prodding required by the University of California Press, which immediately confirmed its intention to publish the book. For her part, Anaïs always wished that everyone she sponsored might be so fortunate.

I know quite well what I received from Anaïs. If I were to presume to guess at what she got from me, I would hope that our friendship was a little sanctuary for her where she could as easily put on a costume as take it off; we laughed a lot together; we played, and we (rarely) cried. I was thirty-two years younger than she, and it is not often that an older woman offers genuine friendship so free of role and hierarchy. I do not believe I was the only one to experience this; my sense is that she found the constraints of rank and status tiresome. Quite frankly, she was my teacher — though never formally — and she was one of the best teachers because, at least with me, she refused to be adored. Particularly in the beginning, her writing influenced my writing profoundly, and who she was influenced and affected my life and my relationships with others. She was a generous woman, and I try to practice that generosity myself.

When she died, I was in New York, fighting, I didn't know then how seriously, for my own life. What I had thought was a battle for the spirit turned out to be a battle for the body as well. As it happens, the very moment she died, I fell down on an icy street just a few hours after discovering I had breast cancer. I like to think it was Anaïs who spoke through the mouth of the elderly black man who commanded two young boys passing by: "Pick that woman up!"

BETTINA KNAPP

Nineteen sixty-six, a momentous year, saw both the publication of *The Diary of Anaïs Nin, 1931-1934* and my meeting with Anaïs — a "universal" woman. Were the two events an example of synchronicity (a meaningful coincidence)? I would like to believe they were.

It all began on a Sunday afternoon. I had just finished reading a review of the *Diary* in *The New York Times*. I was catalyzed into action after learning — much to my surprise and pleasure — that Anaïs had been a friend of Antonin Artaud (1896-1948). Why should Artaud have been so intriguing a figure? Very simply, because I was preparing a book on Artaud at the time.

My next step entailed reading the first volume of Anaïs's *Diary*. I did just that the next day and read it in one sitting. Then I realized that her special understanding and sensitivity to people in general and artists in particular would shed new light on Artaud's personality, thus his ideas and concepts. Different insights would help me better understand Artaud's complexities.

I wrote to Anaïs detailing my project and requested an interview with her. Days later I received an answer, informing me of her imminent departure for her home in Los Angeles and her return to New York some months later. Although terribly busy — she was working on the second and third volumes of her *Diary* and was lecturing around the country — she asked me to write her upon her return, at which time she would grant me a brief interview. Disappointed about the delay, I nevertheless waited patiently.

Following her instructions, I wrote her a second time, at which point Anaïs fixed a time and date for our meeting. It would, she repeated, be short.

I preened for the interview. I wanted to look just right. Having read her *Diary*, I had learned that Anaïs knew a great deal about style; she loved color and was always dressed in an artistic fashion. For financial reasons she frequently made her own clothes and hats. I took great care in choosing what I thought would be just the right outfit to wear for our meeting. I decided on an electric blue suit, a light blue blouse, and shoes to blend. I would wear tiny pearl earrings. Before leaving the apartment, I happened to look out of the window. It seemed like rain. Better to be safe, I reasoned, and so I decided to wear my beige raincoat. One more detail had to be tended to before taking the bus downtown to the New York University neighborhood where she lived. Knowing Anaïs's proclivity for flowers, I decided to buy her a dozen red roses. They looked beautiful in the green wrapping the florist had chosen. Everything was working out perfectly — or almost so.

I finally arrived at my stop, and as I stepped out of the bus there was a cloudburst. Water — propelled by huge gusts of winds — came down from all directions in such quantity that I was drenched in only a few seconds. Worse, as I walked the several blocks to Anaïs's apartment house, I noticed that the color of the once beautiful green papers used by the florist to wrap the roses had run all over my beige raincoat, creating a startlingly weird effect. My eyeliner and mascara — put on with such care only an hour earlier — now covered my cheeks in Rorschach-like configurations. As to my once neatly combed hair, the less said the better.

What to do? Nothing! I knew that Artaud would have been amused and bemused by my predicament. Shorn of all artifice — bereft of my persona — I would have to reveal myself *plain* to Anaïs. A bit anxious and unsure of myself, I rang her doorbell. The door opened. I handed Anaïs what had once been a beautiful bouquet, but now looked far less than enticing, for which she thanked me ever most graciously. No sooner had I heard the timbre of her gentle and richly melodious voice and listened to her words of welcome than my embarrassment was dispelled and I felt at ease.

We sat down almost immediately and began talking. The ten minutes she was to have accorded me turned into four hours of a meaningful and fascinating exchange of ideas revolving around Artaud and his times — the importance the subliminal spheres played in the creative process in general and with regard to the Theater of Cruelty in particular. Anaïs spoke with abandon as she focused on surrealism and the impact it had had on both her life and her writings. Not only did she consider the unconscious as a source of creativity, but also as a force to be used in healing people of their emotional and psychological ailments. What she said was of particular interest to me since Artaud had been associated with the surrealists (1925-27) and their leader, André Breton, who also gave precedence to the unconscious: as in dreams, hallucinations, automatic writing, and other manifestations.

Anaïs empathized with the excitement and yearnings generated by the young surrealists, who had brought forth another and vaster world to be scrutinized, one not limited by rational vision, but infinite, like an inner ocean. With these values and goals in mind, Breton, Louis Aragon, Paul Eluard, Robert Desnos, Max Ernst, and Joan Miró, among others, had succeeded in making themselves, to use Breton's words, "les sourds réceptacles de tant d'échos, les modestes *appareils enregistreurs*" ("the dead receptacles of so many echoes, modest *recording instruments* of another world").[1] Anaïs had known almost all of them, had followed their writings, battles, loves, and obsessions. From them, she had learned to adapt visual/verbal/sonorous motifs to suit her own literary needs — be it in *House of Incest, Winter of Artifice*, or other writings — filling each of her works with her own personal storehouse of riches.

We also talked about D. H. Lawrence, Proust, Woolf, Joyce — the delicacy and sensitivity of their imagery, their penetrating insights, and their extraordinary evocation of moods. If the artistic process is authentic, Anaïs maintained, the work born into the manifest world is an act of courage. It is also an act of aggression that may bring down the wrath of the critics, or worse still, be ignored by the reading public. Artistic expression had become a *modus vivendi* for Anaïs. She realized, as Artaud had already discovered, that creativity was a cruel gift. To create, he had said, was a searing experience, since creation implies alteration. All transformatory processes entail motion and conflict, thus cruelty.

Understandably, Anaïs had repeatedly said that to write a book was to give birth to it, to be delivered of it. In the opening of her *House of Incest* we read: "The morning I got up to begin this book I coughed. Something was coming out of my throat: it was strangling me. I broke the thread which held it and yanked it out. I went back to bed and said: I have just spat out my heart."[2]

She added in a letter to me that writing is fed by subliminal spheres as well as by the world of reality. "The past lives in an invented world, but the quest of the *Diary* and of my life then was for psychological understanding not invention, and this the obsessed poet does not have."[3]

I understood what Anaïs meant only after having completed *Antonin Artaud: Man of Vision,* for which she so kindly agreed to write the preface.

We had many more meetings. Sometimes Anaïs came to visit in our home with Ian Hugo (Hugh Guiler), who showed his films. On several occasions my husband, Russell, took photographs of Anaïs, which she liked very much. We saw each other many times — either at receptions at the Gotham Book Mart or at other literary gatherings.

What amazed me always during the course of the years was that despite Anaïs's tight schedule, and, unbeknown to me, failing health, she was always there for me in time of need — and in times of joy. Whether I needed advice concerning publishers or the placing of articles, generosity was her byword, as was kindness, patience, and understanding. And when good things happened to me — being awarded fellowships, such as the Guggenheim — she would, whether in California, France, or elsewhere, send me a congratulatory telegram or letter, or call me. Firm in her goals, authentic in her approach to people — is it any wonder that a coterie of admirers revolved around her? Anaïs joyed in helping others, as if she were fulfilling a very special act of destiny.

I was not aware of the serious nature of Anaïs's previous bouts with cancer. She rarely if ever mentioned her anguish. In a brief note she wrote *"I am all well,"* assuring me that her energy had returned and that she was at work on the fourth volume of the *Diary.*

Time sped ahead and more operations were in store for Anaïs. Each time she underwent a dismembering procedure, her heroism and her composure revealed a truly adamantine essence.

It was at this time that I undertook to write a book called *Anaïs Nin.*[4] On July 29, 1976, although suffering intensely, she wrote words of encouragement and of praise to me: "I will be very proud of your dedicating a book to me as you know how much I admire your work."[5] And although her usual love of life and in-grained optimism were diminishing, she was still able, as she had always done, to speak openly and truthfully — sometimes about her devastating condition: "I am recovering so slowly that I some-times get a little desperate."[6]

She began another letter in her usual fashion, not thinking of herself but of others first — in this instance, of me. Although her suffering at this time was intense, her attitude toward her disease was first expressed in a positive manner: "I am glad that my ill-ness gives me so much time to read. I can only work 4 or 5 pages a day to finish volume 7."[7] Then she added, with her characteristic refusal to turn aside from objectivity and her equally characteris-tic determination to hold fast to life's bounty:

> About my health it is hard to explain. Radiation has created a fistula (an opening in the stomach) which requires nursing, and I can never leave the house. I wear a bag which has to be emptied and which leaks unexpectedly and then I have to go to bed and wait for the nurse. I explain this because it is the cause of my being locked in. Unless it heals by itself there is no cure. I can't imagine a worse illness for my active temperament. For-tunately, I can work, read. . . .
>
> Aside from health it has been a year of rewards, honors, doc-torates, homages and letters from all over the world, and inter-esting visitors.[8]

When Anaïs departed on January 14, 1977, a beautiful soul flew forth from earth.

NOTES

1. André Breton, "Manifeste du surréalisme," in Breton, *Manifestes du surréalisme* (Paris: Gallimard, 1963), 40. My translation.
2. Anaïs Nin, *House of Incest* (Athens: Swallow Press/Ohio University Press, 1979 [6th printing, 1995]), [1].
3. Letter from Anaïs Nin to Bettina Knapp, 26 December 1968.
4. *Anaïs Nin* (New York: Frederick Ungar, 1978).
5. Letter from Anaïs Nin to Bettina Knapp, 29 July 1976.
6. Ibid.
7. Letter from Anaïs Nin to Bettina Knapp, 28 May 1976.
8. Ibid.

WILLIAM CLAIRE

My first personal encounter with Anaïs Nin took place in the grim basement of St. Mark's Church in New York City, the site of enough literary gatherings to probably qualify it for some sort of historical stone or marker.

The occasion was a sad one; genuine grief over the early death of Alan Swallow, a powerful publishing presence who broke down many barriers that have always separated east from west coast writers. In the basement to remember him were essentially his east coast writers. And Anaïs Nin, whom I didn't know at the time, or where or how she lived.

The first thing that struck me was a radiant and delicate quality that seemed out of place in the bowels of St. Mark's. Her voice lacked, at least from the back of the room, any kind of authority. It had a squeaky, birdlike quality, somewhat effervescent and ethereal, like the clothes she wore. She did not appear to be someone who spent a lot of time in church basements, even one with literary ghosts . . . yet I was aware of her background with the vicarious world of artists and writers, her life on a houseboat, and so forth.

When I chatted with her afterwards (I had merely reviewed many Swallow books, and had not yet begun my magazine) I was properly reticent; I mentioned a vague connection with John Howard Griffin and John F. Mahoney, and something to the effect that I wanted to start a literary magazine someday . . . blah blah blah . . . and wouldn't it be nice if we kept in touch? Or some such.

It would be a year or so later before I would launch my first issue of *Voyages,* in Washington, D.C., during some of the worst fighting of the Vietnam War. The speed with which a few things happened, in retrospect, was part of the history of *Voyages.* And both had to do with people who read at the Swallow memorial. One was Roger Hecht, a Swallow poet, brother of Anthony Hecht, and the other was Anaïs Nin.

I had a wonderful cast of advisory editors, including the legendary and magnificent Mark Van Doren; James Wright, a wonderful poet whose suffering was deep but never on his sleeve; and others. But Roger Hecht and Anaïs Nin were to become my most active advisory editors and friends during the life of *Voyages* and beyond. Nin spent the most time and effort . . . acting like an upwardly eager associate editor gushing with ideas and possibilities for future issues.

A few things should be clear at the outset. No one was ever paid a cent for working on *Voyages,* or for their actual contributions. I am not proud of this; it is simply a fact. No one ever asked for any pay, either. Nor was anyone ever reimbursed for expenses. The result: if anyone wanted to be involved with the magazine at any level during its entire existence, it was a labor of love, and nothing more.

In retrospect, I can conclude a few things. While Anaïs was on board before the first issue, and even helped get a few subscriptions prior to it, I know she was surprised at how impressive the publication looked. This may sound facetious or self-serving, but everyone knows that new literary publications run the gamut from this pre-desktop era of mimeographed manifestoes to established university-type quarterlies and even a few high-tone glossy operations. It's usually a matter of faith to be involved with a publication before its first appearance; what comes out of the tube may not be everyone's baby. In any event, when Nin saw vol. 1, no. 1, with its spectacular cover by Eliot Porter — and the quality of contributors such as Thomas Merton with the first publication of his drawings; Pablo Neruda (thanks to Ben Belitt's translations); the first major interview on the literary programs at the new National Endowment for the Arts, with Carolyn Kizer; and other features — she was ecstatic.

This was at the time when she was emerging as a mainstream figure in literature with the publication of the *Diary*, volume 1, in 1966. From Nin's participatory standpoint and increased pressures on her time, it is easy to conclude that she might have adopted a casual in-name-only advisory role. She had, after all, "made it" after a long, well-documented struggle.

Instead, she became deeply involved with every issue, including an early issue featuring women writers, in 1968. She sent me manuscripts from her friends on both the east and west coasts, and some from abroad. She was my most indefatigable advisory editor throughout the life of the publication, which ended in the early 1970s.

Reflections. Character traits. She never once asked me for anything, or tried to pressure me into publishing any writer. She spent a good bit of her own money and time sending me material, buying subscriptions for friends . . . once even sending me her entire handwritten card files, which I still have. There were constant suggestions, encouragements, meetings together, visits with mutual friends, and, throughout it all, a major belief in the continuity and significance of independent publishing in America and international literature.

Further point. She did not change one iota in her relationship to me or the magazine even after she attained a kind of cult status. If she was filling the house at the Smithsonian Institution, or being feted in the U.S. Supreme Court chambers, she still had time for a "little" magazine.

This has to mean something. I obviously do not have negative things to say about her, and can't be forced into doing so. Of course she was a bit narcissistic; most writers are . . . a commonplace. Of course she felt neglected; I have never met a self-satisfied artist in my life. Real artist, that is.

Some surprising things happened during our long friendship that were related to the peculiar life she lived. I was primarily an east coast friend, and my closest friends were in her east coast world, like Hugo and Anna Balakian. Publishing narrowed the gap between her two worlds; there were endless letters written while in flight between the coasts. And I came to know her west coast friends, too.

I remember with affection the wonderful and astonishly talented people she introduced me to: Gloria and Dan Stern; the late Michael Field, the former pianist become noted food writer; Frances Field; Daisy Aldan; and Harriet Zinnes, among others.

And then there was Valerie Harms, who organized that weekend gathering, with Anaïs present throughout, that has become justifiably part of the Nin lore. As one of the speakers at that Magic Circles' weekend, I was flush with *Voyages* pride and sharing a platform with Anna Balakian and Frances Steloff, whose Gotham Book Mart had been the site of earlier visits with Anaïs. Nor could I conceive then that within a short time span I would be speaking again about Anaïs in that omnipresent circle that death always brings around, if that's what it does. As Emily Dickinson once observed about our often cavalier approach toward friendship, it sometimes gets too late too soon.

At the New York memorial for Nin, I remember our group thinking (I was a late addition to the readers there) that we were again celebrating Nin's life as a writer. We did focus on the work, almost exclusively. And then Joaquín Nin-Culmell came to the podium and began simply with the statement "I loved my sister" and started weeping before he could continue. So too did others weep.

During the Washington, D.C., memorial I organized, we listened to a special tape sent by Henry Miller become very personal and poignant . . . particularly with Hugo sitting in the front row. When Hugo stood and quietly announced to the large gathering in the Cosmos Club that "I should know something about Anaïs; we were married for almost fifty years," a number of people gasped. Speaking before a full house at the Smithsonian Institution in Washington before her illness set in, Anaïs avoided any questions from the floor about her personal life, as though she didn't have one. Some of the people at the memorial had been at the Smithsonian. No wonder they gasped.

Of course the personal life can never be eradicated, but whatever it entails — for the life of the artist in any event — it has to be secondary. With regard to Nin's personal life, of which there continues to be much ado, and much speculation, often inaccurate, I can only say that I have never been troubled by the right of friends to have any private life they choose; if the life she lived offends others, so be it. People have to work that out on their own. Good luck to you, and good luck to me.

Loyalty was her key characteristic. She was loyal to her friends. Perhaps she wanted to get something out of everyone she met. Perhaps. But she also gave a lot . . . in my case, far more than I ever gave her.

To be sure, *Voyages* provided a convenient sounding board for many people who were pressing her with constant demands. It was easier for me to reject manuscripts, after all, than it was for her to do so. She had truly known rejection in her life, and knew that her friends would have to deal with it eventually, too. But she never gave up trying to help others.

More recently, the 1994 Nin conference organized by Suzanne Nalbantian on Long Island brought together another circle of scholars, students, and friends of Nin, including an international contingent. There was Ben Franklin V, with whom I had been in touch over a quarter of a century ago, telling me that *Voyages*, which he probably first heard about from Nin, had been useful in "breaking the ice" for a meeting with Robert Lax, who deserves his own book of tributes. And the first person I talked with, after surviving the highway madness of Long Island on a Memorial Day weekend, was Duane Schneider. Within minutes, we were swapping stories of literature, writing, publishing, mutual friendships set off by Nin like two old fishermen who had lost our nets in many waters. Instantly, the outside world of traffic and travail was forgotten. And I had many talks with Richard Centing, of Ohio State, who did so much to keep the Nin circle together with his publication, *Under the Sign of Pisces*.

Now, as this virtually exhausted century winds to either a dramatic or wimpish end (it could go either way), I worry about our lack of continuity with the past, our increasingly trendy society that outdoes itself in the boredom of the latest fad. Why are there no conferences on the blessed memories of Mark Van Doren, or Thomas Merton, Robert Penn Warren, or Robert Lax? How quickly we forget. And what do we replace them with? No answers here, except to say that for some three decades the life and writings of Anaïs Nin have for a variety of reasons continued to play a role in uniting a group of people, all not necessarily outright admirers, which is fine, too. In the scheme of things, that's not insignificant.

Generosity. Loyalty. Diligence. Belief in the written word, that it might mean something. Spreading the word, widening the circle. When I think of these things, I think of Anaïs Nin. As a local character in these parts says, blessings to her, real good.

Several years ago, while presumably taking notes at an interminable meeting in Washington, I glanced out a boxlike window and saw a random sea gull cavorting about. Now Washington is at least two and a half hours from the Atlantic Ocean where most sea gulls tend to cavort. Washington, meanwhile, is loaded with pigeons. Thinking such thoughts, and strongly identifying with the sea gull and wanting out of the meeting, I started thinking of Anaïs; this was during the time of *Voyages*.

While everyone at the meeting assumed I was working diligently away, I jotted down the following and sent it off to *The Nation* in New York, which published it not too long after and began it on a nice little life of its own among the circle which somewhat amazingly still keeps coming around and around.

THINKING OF ANAÏS NIN

I dream of wayward gulls
and all landless lovers
rare moments of winter sun
peace, privacy, for everyone.[1]

NOTES

1. William Claire, "Thinking of Anaïs Nin," *The Nation*, 29 March 1971: 414.

BENJAMIN FRANKLIN V

In the mid 1960s, I enrolled in the graduate English program at Ohio University. Duane Schneider, a professor with whom I quickly became friendly, recommended a provocatively titled book by an author of whom I had not heard. The book: *House of Incest;* the author, Anaïs Nin. I read the prose poem and was impressed; it struck me as profound, as true. I wanted to read more books like this: writing outside the mainstream, literature not being offered in graduate classes. So I read everything I could by Nin, in editions published by Alan Swallow.

I also wanted to learn about her. I quickly became frustrated trying to discover even the most basic facts, which added to my growing sense of her as something of a mystery woman. I found her mentioned in only a few standard literary reference works, and they contained conflicting information. I recall one source giving her birth date as 1903; another, as 1914.[1] Which was correct, if either? One might have referred to her as Mrs. Ian Hugo, or Mrs. Hugh Guiler. Who were these men? I wanted to know, but I did not know how to proceed. Answers came in time.

In an event that coincided perfectly with my growing interest in — even passion for — Nin, The Swallow Press and Harcourt, Brace & World jointly published the first volume of her *Dairy* in 1966. I recall being attracted to its green-and-black dust jacket and captivated by the pictures of Henry Miller and his wife June, René Allendy, Otto Rank, Antonin Artaud, and, of course, Nin herself. Most of all, I recall reading the text voraciously, at what seemed one sitting. The Nin I met in the *Diary* is the woman I wanted her to be: wild, brave, sensitive, deep, committed. As a bonus, that she had lived in Paris and participated in literary activities there immediately following the departure of the writers known as the Lost Generation added to her mystique. I was hooked, and hooked for life, as it turned out.

Duane and I continued talking about Nin. We looked for writing about her and, aside from a few reviews, found nothing. Realizing that Nin warranted attention, we decided to collaborate on a critical book about her. We were delighted when, after writing to Gunther Stuhlmann, Nin's agent and editor of the *Diary*, Nin herself responded. Her distinctive handwriting charmed me. A regular correspondence ensued. Soon, she invited us to visit her, which we did in March 1967. It turned out to be an ordeal, but one well worth undergoing.

Heavy snow made driving difficult, and conditions worsened in eastern Pennsylvania and New Jersey. They became so bad that the speed limit was lowered to 25 miles per hour. We eventually arrived in New York City and took a room at the Albert Hotel, exhausted but happy at last to be about to meet Nin, which we did that evening.

I think we were nervous as we approached her door at 3 Washington Square Village; we stood in awe of her. We were prepared to be fascinated by someone the likes of whom we had never encountered. She did not disappoint us. Upon opening the door, she greeted us in that odd yet enchanting voice everyone found peculiar, at least upon first hearing it. Is it a French accent? I wondered. Or a mild speech impediment? Whatever it was, I liked it. But what impressed me then and impresses me now, almost a third of a century later, were the words with which she greeted us. She received us as though we had come only a few blocks to see her on a lovely spring day. "Did you have a nice dwive?" "Would you like a dwink?" She seemed oblivious to the length and difficulty of our trip, despite her awareness of the terrible weather conditions we had encountered. Perhaps she was just attempting to put us at our ease and welcome us. She might merely have been nervous at the prospect of meeting us. But asking if we had had a nice drive struck me as bizarre, given the nature of our trip. Her seeming unconcern with worldly realities continued. In response to her second question, I said that I would enjoy a beer. She took a snap-top can from the refrigerator and removed the entire top with a can opener. After speaking pleasantly with us for some time, she placed a folding screen near the door. Shortly thereafter we noticed — we were facing the door — that someone entered, although we could not see the person because of the screen. I saw only a man's brown shoe passing through a small space between the door and the screen. The person, we inferred, was Ian Hugo (Hugh Guiler), who by then we knew was — or had been — Nin's husband. In an effort to conceal the nature of her relationship to him, she had deleted his name from the *Diary;* she continued trying to deny his existence, at least to us. I hope she did not notice our amusement at what struck us as her odd ways.

Duane and I visited Anaïs — for so we then addressed her — in her apartment at least once more, in June 1967. Again she was pleasant and cordial; yet she continued acting strangely, from my point of view. We three dined at a Greenwich Village restaurant. Immediately after being seated, she excused herself in order to make a telephone call, which was lengthy. I recall her eating little. When she commented that we did not drink much wine, I observed that she didn't, either. The glare she directed at me was the first real indication I had that she expected to comment freely on others' behavior but would not permit being commented upon in a manner even mildly critical — and I was merely making conversation. Duane and I were not drinking much, but neither was she. She considered her comment appropriate, but my identical comment inappropriate.

After dinner — or was it before? — I saw her laugh for the only time during our relationship. This happened when, as we were walking in Greenwich Village, I noticed an automobile tail pipe in a street. Because it could have caused a problem for drivers, I did what I thought anyone would do: I stepped into the street to remove it. Apparently the tail pipe had just fallen from a car, because when I picked it up it was hot — so hot that I dropped it and kicked it to the side of the street. To her, this was uproariously funny. I don't think she doubled over, but she laughed out loud. She apparently thought that only a hopeless rube would attempt to help Manhattan traffic move smoothly, and anyone attempting to do so deserved being burned. I did not find this amusing.

She revealed another aspect of her personality to me in 1973 when she was in Ann Arbor to lecture at the University of Michigan, where I was teaching. As I drove her to my home for dinner, she became uneasy. Although I had told her that the gathering would be low-key and that in addition to the two of us the only people there would be Duane, my wife, our elder daughter, and my sister-in-law, she began questioning me almost frantically about people with whom she would be spending time. I repeated what I had told her earlier and tried my best to calm her. But how strange that this woman who would captivate a large audience for an hour without using notes would fear having dinner with a few people, some of whom she knew, and all of whom wished only for her comfort. Although she was pleasant at dinner, once again she ate little, despite the elegant meal Jo, my wife, had prepared.

Practically from the beginning, Anaïs and I had a strained relationship, although it was usually outwardly friendly. Our personalities did not mesh. I know I irritated her. I did so because my interest in her had been and would remain academic, scholarly, despite, in the early years, being also attracted by her personality and the life she had led. I pestered her because I thought she could help me account for her various publications, some of which I assumed must have appeared only in ephemeral little magazines. I preferred knowing what she had written before writing about her work. At least initially she fielded my questions with good humor, although, to tell the truth, she was not much help. Here is one example. From a source I do not now recall, I learned that she had written a story entitled "Mischa's Confession to the Analyst." Because I found no reference to it in the usual bibliographical sources and could not verify its existence, I asked her about it. She said she had written no such story. Within a few days of receiving her answer, I discovered, serendipitously, this very story by her in the journal *Seven* in the University of Michigan library. In time, I became comfortable with the details of her publishing career and published a bibliography of her works with the Kent State University Press in 1973. When she received a copy, she seemed pleased with my effort.

Our relationship finally concluded as a result of my writing for *Under the Sign of Pisces: Anaïs Nin and Her Circle,* a newsletter published at Ohio State University and edited by Richard Centing and me. It ended because of my comments in *Pisces* about a collection of Anaïs's books being offered for sale by a book dealer. I criticized him for claiming to offer the complete Nin first editions when he did not. I could not have foreseen the ramifications of this piece, which was factual, not interpretive. I carelessly stated that the book dealer had "hoodwinked" prospective buyers with his claim of completeness. Offended, he threatened to sue Ohio State because I had defamed him in a journal it published. In the end, nothing came of this because I apologized in print for having used so inappropriate a word.

Unbeknown to me, Anaïs was negotiating with this man to publish selections from her work in a book that would be handsomely designed and bound. She thought my dispute with him placed this book deal in jeopardy, as it had also jeopardized the newsletter. In the end, the book was published — indeed, it is handsome — and the newsletter survived this crisis. But I was out. Anaïs, who had had enough of me and my independent ways, apparently asked Centing to remove me as editor of *Pisces,* which he did. She wished to control what was written about her.

Anaïs wanted badly to have her work studied in colleges and universities. Several times I taught her works at Michigan in a Nin/Henry Miller seminar; other professors taught her work elsewhere. But she seemed unaware that she had to pay a price for such exposure, and the price was criticism. Professors and students do not just retell the plot of a piece of literature and then swoon over its sublimity; they analyze it, praising some aspects of it and criticizing others. Such responses occasionally reach a larger audience through articles and books of criticism. Anaïs seemed oblivious to this reality. In fact, the worst thing she could call someone was an intellectual, by which she meant a person detached and analytical, as professors are trained to be; she preferred intimacy and unquestioning acceptance. On more than one occasion she called me an intellectual, which, according to her use of the word, I was, and perhaps am. Although I fully understood that in so characterizing me she had intended to insult me, I was not insulted. Rather, I felt a certain pride in having been able to keep my integrity in the face of the powerful personality of a woman who wished to be studied but not criticized.

When I had been seriously ill in 1969 and 1970, Anaïs had been concerned enough to telephone me in the hospital, a gesture I greatly appreciated. When I learned in 1976 that she was similarly confined, and possibly terminally ill, I wrote to her. (We had not recently corresponded.) I don't know if she received my letter. She did not respond to it, possibly because she was too ill to do so. Perhaps she did not wish to renew contact with me. Yet I have always been glad I wrote to her. She was a woman who had been and would continue being important to me, and I wished to express my genuine concern and support for her.

Because Anaïs died from her illness in 1977, she did not live to see the book Duane and I wrote about her, which was not published until 1979. Because we focused only on her literary creations and pointed out what struck us as her strengths as well as her weaknesses, I doubt that she would have liked it. She would therefore have seen me as having betrayed her once more, and she would not have been surprised.

But she would be surprised that I, a person she rejected as being detrimental to her career, have edited *Recollections of Anaïs Nin*. And how ironic that at the time I contracted to edit this book, the director of the Ohio University Press was Duane Schneider, the person who introduced me to Nin's work and who became my partner in crime in writing *Anaïs Nin: An Introduction*. Our interest in Anaïs began three decades ago, and it continues. I shudder to think how she would respond to this new book.

NOTES

1. On my office wall hangs a 1976 poster of Nin (published by Les Femmes) which includes the following: *"Anaïs Nin/1914- ."* She was born in 1903.

DUANE SCHNEIDER

Living in Colorado in the early 1960s, I pursued a Ph.D. in literature and would try to keep myself sane by taking a break from
normal studies by reading all that I could of a single author. One
of these was John Steinbeck. Another was Henry Miller. It was
during my reading of Miller that I came across the description of
work by an intriguing character with the curious name, Anaïs
Nin. I moved to a faculty position in Ohio, and once I finished
reading all the Miller I could find, I turned to Nin's *Under a Glass
Bell* (which I liked well enough, and understood), *House of Incest*
(which I didn't know whether to like or not, and which I did not
understand), and a third book, the title of which I have now forgotten.

I spoke to my friend Ben Franklin about these works and for
some reason he, too, wanted to read them; at someone's suggestion — perhaps mine — I gladly traded him three Nin books for
one by Thomas Wolfe, since I was in the process of building a
huge collection of Wolfe's books. This transaction in 1966 was to
be the beginning of a series of events that brought Anaïs Nin into
our lives for the next ten years and put us in touch with her works
to this day.

By November 1966, Ben and I had a contract with a commercial publisher to write a book on Anaïs's works; since inevitable
questions were arising, both bibliographical and critical, we were
soon writing to Anaïs via her agent, Gunther Stuhlmann. We
found Anaïs to be a very willing and cooperative correspondent,

for she indicated that no book had as yet been written about her works. Our correspondence grew during early 1967, though in a somewhat awkward and cumbersome way. Ben and I would write her jointly, I with one set of questions and comments, he with another. She would write us jointly at the English Department of Ohio University, Athens. Our epistolary friendship grew, and soon we were talking on the telephone; then it was determined that we would pay her a visit in New York during March 1967. This was to be the first of six or seven face-to-face encounters I had with Anaïs during the late 1960s and early 1970s.

After driving all night from Ohio through heavy snow, we arrived in Manhattan early in the morning of Friday, March 17, and checked into the Albert Hotel, Thomas Wolfe's old haunt, a hotel in 1967 still closely affiliated with New York University, full of students, all-night saxophones, bathroom down the hall. We arrived at Anaïs's apartment in Washington Square Village in the early evening.

As we approached her apartment on the fourteenth floor I was beside myself: I was hoping desperately that she would be more a beautiful young woman than an unattractive old lady. By the time Ben and I made it all the way down the hall past apartments 14 H, G, F, E, D, C, to A and B, it was (I'm now astonished to say) too much for me. I couldn't carry through with it. I walked all the way back to the elevator area to fill my pipe with good rich tobacco. Finally to her door, where we rang the doorbell. I didn't look at Ben. He didn't look at me. It was too much for both of us. Almost immediately she appeared, all of a light sandalwood color — light beige dress, a beautiful woman with a slight figure and a slim waist, full skirt, complexion very fair, auburn hair, a good deal of mascara. Altogether, extremely attractive.

She shook our hands and welcomed us. We discarded our coats and sat down on Danish modern furniture, the kind so popular in this country at that time. She asked us about the blizzard, offered us drinks. After she brought us our drinks (Scotch for me, beer for Ben) she cleared the air by asking the most important question of the evening: Will our book be about her writings or will some of it be biographical? I assured her that we would be writing about her works and not about her — which is what we intended, and which is what we did. She was clearly delighted and indicated that she then could speak more candidly. I described the New Critical approach we would take toward her work (also a sign of the times), and though she hadn't heard of New Criticism, she expressed both favor and relief, because it is a critical approach that focuses on the writing and not the writer. This concern — whether our book would contain, as she put it, "any personal biographical information" — crops up later more than once in her correspondence to us.

Then she told us of her Freudian slip. Although she had written us that ours would be the first book about her works, we heard (to our bewilderment) that Oliver Evans had already written a study of them for Harry T. Moore's Crosscurrents series at Southern Illinois University Press, although she didn't like what he had written. She *wished* that ours would be the first such study to be published. We were somewhat cheered at the possibility of having our book in print before Oliver Evans's, but it was not to be.

Our conversation turned to Alan Swallow, whom she admired greatly. And to Hugo and his works. Soon Anaïs went to shut a screen because soon her husband would be home. And later, to our great interest and delight, Hugo appeared, but we got only a glimpse of him, the Great Missing Character from the first volume of the published *Diary*. While Anaïs refreshed our drinks, we looked around. On the walls were a permanent screen for viewing Hugo's films; copper Hugo engravings illuminated by red, white and blue lights; and a huge Varda collage. On a table were some dried flowers. It was all much better, more colorful, and exciting than we had expected. Anaïs was consistently receptive, generous, and cordial, if a bit restrained. And yet she was open with us and did not evade any of our questions. Her cooperation made us feel that we could count on her to help us out as needed when we would begin to explicate the texts of her work.

We pursued other topics, such as how we could locate and possibly buy such rare items as *The Booster* and *Delta*. Anaïs telephoned Frances Steloff at the Gotham Book Mart; although the shop was not open, Miss Steloff was working late and tried to help us.

Instead of going out for dinner and returning to her apartment, we decided to stay on a bit longer. She and I discussed a publication of hers I wanted to produce, and eventually did, on a handpress bought from Ben's father. Ben asked about Varda, Val Telberg, and Alfred Perlès. I asked her about her brothers. I had talked with Joaquín on the telephone and found him cordial. She did not want to discuss Thorvald; she simply indicated that he was a retired businessman and that they had never been very close. Soon Anaïs had to make a long distance telephone call. She made long distance calls every time I visited her apartment.

Anaïs inscribed some books for us and invited us to come back to New York in June for a party celebrating the publication of the second volume of her *Diary*. She began to tire, so we prepared to leave. "Should we keep writing you through Gunther Stuhlmann?" "No, write directly, either in New York or Los Angeles." She suggested that we visit her in Los Angeles, too, since Ohio (she thought) was mid-point between New York and the West coast. This kind of ingenuousness (similar to opening the entire lid of Ben's snap-top can of beer with an electric can opener) was displayed so openly and honestly that one truly did not know how to respond to it.

Back to the Albert and to bed after a magnificent evening.

In addition to seeing her at the publishing party in June, I saw Anaïs again in June 1969 when I interviewed her for a small book I published, and I saw her in Ann Arbor when she spoke there in 1973. In March 1968 I had assigned some of her works to a class studying fiction, and she generously allowed us to telephone her in New York from our Ohio University classroom. A number of these undergraduates asked her questions about what they had read, questions that were quite appropriate. Anaïs answered with patience, understanding, and intelligence. The inevitable one surfaced: "Miss Nin, would you comment on the degree of autobiography that occurs in *Under a Glass Bell?*" I have regretted for many years that I did not record the entire exchange that day.

In 1967, Anaïs wrote me that "Miller is in Japan with an exhibition of his water colors. By the way, a penurious poet wants to sell a water color Henry Miller gave him (anonymous). If you know anyone who would want it the price is 50 dollars."[1] I have been the happy owner of that Henry Miller watercolor ever since.

Anaïs paid great attention to detail, especially where her work was the subject of discussion. I had to justify the use of the word *bizarre* regarding some of Sabina's love affairs. And when I used the word *lurid* to describe the cover of the Avon *Spy in the House of Love,* I heard about that, too. When I was focusing on the persona of Anaïs Nin in the *Diary,* I indicated that "we are left, finally, with the definition of a single, primary, multi-faceted character, Anaïs Nin";[2] her response — which I found surprising — was "You don't mean that you do not get the portraits of Miller, Artaud[,] Rank[,] etc[.]?"[3] (I responded that it was *primarily* her portrait that emerged.) Truth to tell, I found her to be on the whole generous, human, warm, responsive, and above all a lively correspondent during the years of 1967–76.

In 1968 Anaïs wrote to Ben: "I'm glad your efforts were responded to. I owe you both so much. You have the same definition of friendship I have: you are active about what you care for! I never understood a passive love of anything."[4] And from my favorite letter of all from March 30, 1967: "Dear Friends: I think of you as a partnership. . . . I like your enthusiasm. It is my favorite quality. If I had answered Proust's famous questionnaire: which is your favorite flower, etc. I would say enthusiasm! It brings things to life."[5]

Anaïs wrote me last in August 1976, a few months before she died; and although she was too weak to leave the house, her letter nonetheless was one that evinced strength, hope, and courage.

NOTES

1. Letter from Anaïs Nin to Duane Schneider, 23 August 1967.
2. Duane Schneider, "The Art of Anaïs Nin," *The Southern Review* 6 (April 1970): 514.

3. Letter from Anaïs Nin to Duane Schneider, 1 December 1967. Nin responds to a typescript of my essay.

4. Letter from Anaïs Nin to Benjamin Franklin V, 13 December 1968.

5. Letter from Anaïs Nin to Benjamin Franklin V and Duane Schneider, 30 March 1967.

ROBERT ZALLER / LILI BITA

Text in roman type by Robert Zaller.
Text in italic type by Lili Bita.

I first encountered Anaïs Nin in the slender editions of her novels that Alan Swallow put out in the 1960s. Later I found an old copy of the record she'd made reading from *Under a Glass Bell*, and the distant, liquid voice became inseparable for me from the text itself — I heard Anaïs as I read her. And read her as one reads an author one feels one has found for oneself and does not particularly wish to share with another.

I did share Anaïs finally, with Lili, and that simple but for me weighty gesture — "I have a book I think you'd like to read" — set much more in motion than I knew. Lili's reaction was not to prize Anaïs; she insisted on meeting her.

"That's impossible," I said. Anaïs Nin was in fact no longer a private property; the first volume of the *Diary* had already been published, and fame, at sixty-three, had arrived for her. There were interviews, readings, lectures, the impedimenta of renown. No longer the object of a cult, Anaïs was on her way to becoming a religion. One did not meet such a person; one did not wish to, as if the commerce of such an occasion must somehow embarrass both parties.

"The best of a writer goes into her books," I said. "You aren't missing anything."

Fortunately, Lili ignored me.

Anaïs Nin seemed to speak my own language in a foreign tongue. Not my native Greek, but a private, inner speech no one had ever guessed at before. I read without stopping, incapable of

*stopping, running through periods and paragraphs, brushing
aside the unfamiliar vocabulary — there would be time enough
for the dictionary later — borne along on a wave of music more
than of words, the elation of finding a woman who spoke directly
to me as a woman. The words would not suffice. I felt impelled to
meet not the author merely, but the woman herself.*

*How was it to be done? Not as a fellow writer (I knew nothing
then of the generosity with which Anaïs nurtured young artists),
surely not as a mere admirer (I knew nothing either of the patience with which she tried to answer every correspondent). Why
then not act on my first, immediate impulse? I wanted to share
Anaïs Nin with other Greek women. Why not do so?*

*I approached the editor of a local Greek paper, who agreed to
the idea of an interview with Anaïs. I phoned her agent, Gunther
Stuhlmann. Stuhlmann was polite but unencouraging. I must
understand the pressure of Miss Nin's commitments, the piles of
correspondence, the deluge of requests. My message would be
conveyed, but I must not expect a speedy reply, nor a favorable
one. I hung up, dashed.*

*A month later, Anaïs rang. In her high, girlish voice she said
she would very willingly be introduced to the Greek public. Would
I like to come over to her apartment next evening?*

Lili put off her interview for a few days, while I attended to
Ph.D. orals out of town. Curiosity overcame conviction, and I
joined her for lunch at Anaïs's Greenwich Village apartment. We
had, I think, the same instant impression of meeting a wise, rare
fowl. Anaïs spoke directly, with few gestures; her smiles were brief
and unornamented. Action and reticence seemed to war in her. It
was not that she was in the least hesitant or indecisive, but that
her movements did not carry through, as if robbed of their force.
One could tell — even see — that the initial impulse behind them
was always greater than the result. Only in speaking did she seem
without reserve. Yet at the same time there was something light
and almost mercurial about her, and it seemed difficult to conceive the kind of weight that could pin down so aerial a creature.

Lili had come to interview, but she stayed to confess. It was as
if one of Anaïs's own characters had suddenly leaped into the
room, demanding to know why she had been created thus and

61

thus; I understood then how intensely Lili had identified with them.

Anaïs was waiting for us down the long corridor to her apartment. We embraced without preliminaries, as if we were old friends who had known one another for years. I felt her body, light and pliant, through her long purple chemise. "Purple," she said, "is my color."

My impression was of large green eyes and red lips, alert antennae in a pale, heart-shaped face. A restrained coquetry that belied the woman of sixty-five, an Old World desire to charm and please. I recognized a fellow European.

We sat together on the sofa, not needing or wanting distance between us. Varda's collage "Women Reconstructing the World" occupied a wall of the parlor. Anaïs spoke of Varda's vitality and exuberance, the influence of his Greek roots. "I dream of visiting your Greece," she told me. "The myth, the color, the ambience have all touched my writing."

Our talk went on. The afternoon faded. Anaïs brought a tray of refreshments, coffee and biscuits. I tapped my notebook dutifully: "The interview," I said. "We'd better begin."

"Another time," Anaïs replied, as if we both knew the pretext of the visit was no longer necessary. "First, I'd like to know more about the person I am going to confide my life to."

We saw Anaïs twice again that spring before she left to lecture in California, and we met Hugo, too. He was gracious but diffident, a tall, elderly man with a Somerset Maughamish air, like an English gentleman retired on Hinduism and yoga. Probably his attire suggested the connection: a Nehru jacket with a large crystal pendant. Hugo was only five years Anaïs's senior, but he seemed to belong to a different generation; and indeed Anaïs whispered to us: "He is my father." The relationship, she intimated, was one of sufferance. So it appeared. Hugo was somehow a stranger in his own home, a guest who had tarried in the hope of being taken for a resident. That he worshipped Anaïs was clear, but he had been trained out of any gesture of intimacy, and wore a sad, thwarted air. Yet he remained heartbreakingly loyal. After forty-five years of marriage, he still hoped for affection from his wife.

We asked about Hugo's absence from the published *Diary.*

Anaïs replied that she had altered many identities to protect living persons, but that in Hugo's case concealment was impossible: he would have to be either all in or all out, and he had agreed himself that the latter course was preferable. With the publication of the "unexpurgated" diaries the issues have, of course, become clearer. But it seemed even then that Hugo's effacement was more a matter of erasure than of tact. When the later volumes of the original set appeared, Anaïs justified the evasion of her relationship with Rupert Pole on the same ground of protecting Hugo. "He knows nothing of what it really is," she told us: "It would kill him if he ever found out."

I found this hard to believe; the tension was palpable whenever Anaïs set out for California. What was apparent was that it was no longer a subject for discussion, if it ever had been.

Anaïs took me into her bedroom. I'd expected a cluster of rich French scents and creams on her dressing table, but there was only a facial steamer and a drugstore jar of Pond's lotion. Anaïs showed me a small statuette of Venus, a votive offering, sent by an admirer.

The diaries were ranged on a shelf, bound and numbered, meticulously ordered.

"I'd like to read them all, cover to cover," I said.

"Yes," Anaïs replied, noncommittally, "The truth is there."

I took a breath.

"But aren't the published ones the truth?"

"Oh, the truth, yes, but . . . modified."

"How do you mean?"

"Well, take the story of Gonzalo and Helba. Gonzalo was not a friend but a lover. We had a very intense affair. He was terribly jealous, even violent."

"But what about Helba? Your kindness toward her, the trips to the hospital . . ."

"I hated her," Anaïs said. "She ruined Gonzalo, destroyed him. Years ago I went back to visit them in Paris. Gonzalo was dead, and Helba was in a home. I wished she had died instead."

"But in the Diary *she seems to be your sister . . ."*

Anaïs had moved on, however. "What I said just before in front of Hugo about a hideaway in California where I live and work alone isn't true either. It's a home where I live with someone else.

*He looks like a younger Hugo; he could actually be his son.
You'll meet him when you come to California."*

Anaïs gave me a phone number and an address. "Keep this a
secret." she added.

I left shaken. Was the Diary *a lie? Or the confession I'd just
heard? Did the truth lie elsewhere still?*

That fall, I invited Anaïs to lecture at the University of California, Santa Barbara, where I was teaching. The schedule was
heavy and we took her home for a rest in the afternoon. Anaïs
wrapped herself in Lili's robe, but complained of a chill; we had
to raise the thermostat to 80 degrees before she got comfortable.
With interviewers and audiences, she was composed and quietly
commanding — it was clear that attention was an elixir to her,
after decades of neglect — but the toll on her energies was evident.
It was only later that we learned she was already ill, and facing
surgery. Illness was not something of which she spoke; it was
another of her secrets.

The lecture was a redaction of *The Novel of the Future*, which
had just been published. It was the first of Anaïs's books that had
disappointed me; the self-justification that occasionally marred
the *Diary* was more concentrated, the quarrel with unfriendly
critics more overt. Delivered in the sweet chime of her own voice,
however, the argument seemed less tendentious than in print.
The audience, overflowing the hall, was rapt. At the reception af-
terward, Anaïs was besieged by admirers.

"This must be a satisfying time for you," I suggested. "To arrive finally, to be recognized, sought after, to feel your words
connect."

"No," Anaïs said. "It's not like that at all."

*Rupert Pole drove up later in the day and met us at the lecture.
He stood protectively near Anaïs, guarding her like a precious
icon that must not be exposed too long to the enthusiasm of the
faithful. After the reception, we invited them to come back for a
nightcap. Rupert declined, politely but firmly.*

"It's time for us to go home."

*

Rupert was still in the background when we visited Anaïs in Los Angeles. Their house, set on a hill in the Silver Lake district, looked down on the city. There was a Japanese simplicity to the interior, and, to the right of the swimming pool outside, a small, wrought-iron pagoda: "To exorcise evil spirits," Anaïs said. She *served us herself, with the graciousness and elegance of a woman bred to please.*

There were other reasons for Anaïs's ambivalence about her new celebrity besides the suspicion that it would not last. Clearly more at home here domestically than in her apartment in New York, she was also farther from her French cultural roots. The Japanese decor was only a partial compensation.

"There's no common ground between the sexes in America," she lamented. *"Men and women really hate each other here. It shows up in conversation, in manners, in the competition you see in business life. It's all negativity, all ugliness, all prospering at someone else's expense."*

Anaïs seemed at that moment to belong not merely to another continent and culture, but to another era. What, in truth, did she make of the unisex couples of Aquarius who thronged to hear her, but were perhaps ultimately not very different from the angry young professionals who fought for the corner office?

The weather was hot. Anaïs suggested a swim. "I didn't bring a suit," I said.

"Oh, we can swim nude," Anaïs replied. "Or I can give you Renate's swimsuit."

To swim in the costume of one of Anaïs's heroines, Renate Druks, seemed an even more intimate gesture than nudity. It was sizes too small, but somehow I squeezed into it. We laughed at the effect, and Anaïs went to fetch a camera. She wore a bikini that outlined her huntress's body, a body that despite its eunuch-like presentation in the Diary, *had given and received much pleasure, and seemed still avid to do so.*

*

The tact and generosity of Anaïs's friendship was like an aura of care. Notes of encouragement, suggestions for venues, and en-

trees to agents and publishers she'd contacted on our behalf came on a sometimes weekly basis. When Anaïs noticed that I wasn't wearing a watch, she bought me one. When my coat looked threadbare, she brought back a poncho from Mexico. Her gifts were practical, but they were even more important to me as talismans, tokens of a somehow tutelary regard. They sheltered me.

When a book of my poems was about to appear, Anaïs volunteered a preface. A week later she called to read what she'd written. I tried to stammer my gratitude, but Anaïs was only anxious to know if she'd pleased me and caught the spirit of my work. I felt humbled before the woman who had humbled herself to me.

I made the only recompense I could. I'd promised to introduce Anaïs to the Greek public by way of an interview. Now I set out to translate her work into my own tongue for the first time. I chose A Spy in the House of Love, *the most accessible of her novels, I thought, and one I felt a particular kinship toward. Robert and I had rented a summer house on the Greek island of Kythera, fittingly a place sacred to Aphrodite. The veranda gave out on a magnificent view of the harbor and the surrounding coast. Each day I worked from sunup to dusk; each evening we walked uphill by flashlight to get our supper in the village. For nineteen days I lived Sabina's labyrinthine life. When the work was done I sent a telegram, and we went to the village to celebrate. Anaïs inscribed the telegram in her* Diary. *Knowing I'd receive no royalties from the Greek publisher, she agreed to forgo her own and sent me a check for her share.*

Anaïs did not feel well-served by the one book of criticism about her in print, Oliver Evans's. The various shorter essays and prefaces that had appeared over the years were widely scattered, as was the new criticism of the *Diary*. Need and opportunity seemed well met. I decided to compile *A Casebook on Anaïs Nin*.

Anaïs herself entered enthusiastically into the project, opening up her files and suggesting scholars interested in her work. A publisher, World, preferred a contract. Could a book go so smoothly?

It couldn't. My editors at World changed with bewildering rapidity, and the New York office, each time I visited it, seemed smaller and smaller. At last I was assigned someone who greeted me with the smile of an estate auditor.

"Now," he began, "tell me: Who is Anaïs Nin?"

As World foundered, we wondered whether we could free ourselves from the contract. These days, of course, such experiences
are commonplace — and usually far more brutal and direct — but
the corporate takeover of publishing was still a new thing then,
and I was novice enough not to realize how enserfed an author
was.

In the end, we were relatively lucky. A letter arrived one day to
inform me that my contract had been transferred to the New
American Library. The book was produced as carelessly as possible, and ditched onto the market. Against all odds, it survived.

*

Anaïs herself was haunted by the sense that her celebrity was
transient and her reputation insecure. Slights and betrayals were
accordingly magnified in her eyes, and she could be bitter about
those who had misused her. There was a very unpleasant meeting
with Gore Vidal, once a protégé, who had just satirized her in
Two Sisters. Literary license protected Vidal, but Anaïs herself
was obliged to get personal permission to include material about
him in the fourth volume of the *Diary*. They met in a café, and
Vidal proposed lunch. Anaïs confronted him with his novel; Vidal
heatedly denied having based the portrait of Maria on her. There
was no lunch.

I suggested that Anaïs ignore Vidal's fleabite; "Anyway," I
said, "he is a mediocre novelist."

"Yes," Anaïs replied. "You know, when I first met Vidal, he
was struggling to write, to escape his mother, who told him he
had no talent. I supported him, I championed him, I gave him
confidence. But you know, his mother was right."

*

In retrospect I think that in some ways Lili was Anaïs's last
heroine, the last version of the freer, more spontaneous, more
hectically beautiful, yet also more conflicted and divided self that
she approached in the incessant revisions of her art. There were
passionate seances — I don't know what else to call them — in

which she wrestled with the demons of Lili's soul, healer and supplicant at once. The contradictions of Anaïs's life and art, some of which shocked and pained us, must be seen in that light. To please, and to pretend in order to please, and somewhere in between to take life in deep, swift draughts — isn't this the very paradigm of art itself? The integrity of Anaïs's life was in the quest, not in the fables with which she marked her way. Hers was the art of the labyrinth. Let those who wish straight roads and clear destinations walk another way.

Late in her illness, we visited Anaïs — for the last time, as it turned out — in Los Angeles. She lay on a chaise in a vivid yellow dress set off by a blue necklace. Baby-fine hair, newly grown, was just lengthening past her ears. Suffering had not aged but in a curious sense rejuvenated her, bringing back an earlier, younger face. She talked about a healer who had come to her, infusing energy into her limbs; "I felt a surge of great warmth, an urge to rise and fly," she said. Which flight she was preparing for she did not say, but she talked, for us, about the future.

Rupert gently lifted her as we took our leave. She managed to stand in his arms.

"Next summer in Greece, I'll teach you to dance," I said.

Anaïs smiled and lifted her hand.

"I'd like that very much."

JOHN FERRONE

When an author and editor get along and trust each other everybody benefits — the author, the editor, and the publisher, as well as the object of their collaboration, the author's book. This doesn't always happen. Editors routinely deal with demanding, unappreciative authors, or they help build an author's reputation only to have him defect to another publishing house when he hits the jackpot. Authors can be faced with a lazy or inefficient editor, an editor who decides to make a career move when an author's book is in midstream, or one who is more interested in climbing the corporate ladder than in repairing manuscripts. Anaïs Nin and I were lucky. I gave her the devoted editorial care she needed and deserved. She gave me eight of the most rewarding years of my publishing experience.

Our cordial first meeting deepened into affection. In due course I was admitted into the mysteries of her double life. She had already extracted all there was to know about me. We were soon sharing domestic as well as professional concerns. If she expected unconditional loyalty from me, she was ready to offer as much. I learned this when my position at Harcourt Brace Jovanovich became shaky in 1975 and I faced the prospect of changing jobs. Anaïs was quick to explore any contractual restraints that would prevent her following me. It is not uncommon for an author to join a migrating editor at a new house, but Anaïs would have orphaned five of her *Diary* volumes, and so a move of that kind was a very serious one.

Recollections of Anaïs Nin

We were friends from the moment she stood in the doorway of my office in 1969, dressed in white from head to toe. I fell for it all — the kohled green eyes, the dazzling costume, the softly rolled French *r*. She had come to plead for a revised cover on the newly published paperback edition of her *Diary*. She got it. A front-page *New York Times* review in 1966 had given her literary sanction. Now paperback distribution would give her an audience. It was exhilarating to witness Anaïs Nin in the act of becoming famous. Many authors keep fame to themselves. Anaïs shared it, largely through a prodigious correspondence. As her appearances on college campuses increased, so did the flow of her letters and purple postcards. She kept us up to date on her lecture schedules, told us who was "teaching" her *Diary*, asked for books to be sent to impecunious readers, announced the honors being heaped on her. Along with this came frequent supplications on behalf of artists, photographers, and other writers. Would I be interested in publishing Marianne Greenwood's photographs of Picasso? John Boyce's erotic drawings? a good woman poet? Harold Norse's memories? James Leo Herlihy's? a book by Lloyd Wright? the last two volumes of Edgard Varèse's biography? Tristine Rainer's book on diary writing? Marguerite Young's neglected masterpiece? (Yes, I said to the last two and succeeded in publishing the second.) She confessed to pushing a cause now and then out of worry over a friend's poverty.

When I became her official editor, after the death of Hiram Haydn, we edited by mail, since she lived in Los Angeles most of the year and I was based in New York. For the first time I was not just reprinting her books but working with her on diary manuscripts. Authors vary sharply in their ability to accept direction, and I didn't know what to expect of Anaïs; but for someone who was supposed to be touchy about her prose, she was surprisingly responsive to editorial nitpicking. Editing in itself was not the problem, she once explained, but her quest for perfection and annoyance at her own failure. Whatever it was, she rallied nicely and even resigned herself to the tedious business of clearing diary material for our legal hounds. I made a speech to her about being the perfect author. But occasionally she balked, and in 1975 while undergoing a course of chemotherapy her customary good humor began to wear thin. We were going over the manuscript for volume six of the *Diary*, and after several rounds of queries she complained that I was overtaxing her. She needed her limited energy to start on a "beautiful" volume seven. Please, she wrote, no more changes; and please, I must stop giving her so much extra work. I felt wretched. She made up for it a few weeks later by saying, "We have had the only loving association between writer and publisher." (She often made the mistake of calling me her publisher.)

By this time Rupert Pole was helping her prepare the *Diary* for publication. I paid them a visit in February of 1976, shortly after Anaïs's seventy-third birthday, and was shocked to see how much she had deteriorated since the previous April. Among other things we discussed the ending for what would become the final volume of the *Diary*. I wanted her to include some of the hospital experiences she had told me about and which she recorded in a separate part of the diary labeled "The Book of Pain." I remember her saying rather bitterly, "I have shown people how to live. Must I show them how to die, too?" There were few direct communications with her the rest of the year, although Rupert passed along messages. A last letter came from her at the end of October. It was handwritten, the writing sure, with just one correction, of the word "crisis." She spoke of progress on volume seven of the *Diary*, and of Rupert reading to her at all hours because the pain-killers she was taking blurred her vision. Writing to me must have cost her precious strength, and one could almost hear her sigh as she wrote her closing line, "Well, I managed at least a letter!"

On January 13, 1977 I went to the National Book Critics Circle Awards ceremony in the Time-Life auditorium in Rockefeller Center. Anaïs was on my mind throughout the event, and when I got home I wanted to tell her about it. Knowing how difficult it was for her to read, I decided to tape a letter she could listen to. I did part of it that evening and planned to add to it later. She died the next night, and so the letter was never sent. I am sending it now.

Anaïs, I thought I'd send you a letter this way for a change. I just came back from the National Book Critics Circle Awards ceremony this evening, and I found myself talking mostly about you. Nona Balakian was there — she's one of the judges — and I met Anna Balakian for the first time. She said you are constantly saying to her, "Go and see John Ferrone. You're neglecting your work" — meaning, I think, you believe that some of it ought to be in paperback. And I said to her, "Isn't it so like Anaïs to be still worrying about everybody else." She's coming to the office one day, and I don't know what I can do at this point, considering certain pressures on me to turn out more popular fare in paperback, but let's see what happens.

I also talked about you with one of the award winners, a Chinese-American woman named Maxine Hong Kingston, who wrote a book called *Woman Warrior*, which has startled the publishing world. I've just begun reading it. So far, I can say it's an extremely beautiful, moving book. It's about her own life — the difficulty in straddling two cultures, Chinese and American, particularly the difficulties for a woman. It's a book you'd be very much interested in. I'll send it to you as soon as I've finished it, and have Rupert read it to you. I wish you could meet Maxine. She's a charming woman. She lives in Honolulu. She flew in for this occasion with her husband and young son, who is about nine or ten. She's a tiny creature, about four feet eight, I'd say, in her middle forties, with long, straight black hair with a bit of gray in it, and she seemed to be entirely unmoved by all the fuss about her — completely truthful, straightforward — and I enjoyed my few minutes' conversation with her. When I read in the *Times* around Christmas that Maxine Hong Kingston was a great admirer of yours I immediately took the opportunity to write to her and ask if she would consider reading the erotica [*Delta of Venus*] and giving us an advance quote. To my delight she wrote back very promptly and said yes, so I sent it off to her. This evening I asked if she had read it, and she said she had, but hadn't had a chance yet to set anything down. So I said, "Did it curl your hair?" She laughed and said, "Well, it did a bit. Maybe I can say that. 'It curled my hair.'" She was so pleased to be meeting Anaïs Nin's editor, I had to remind her that she was the celebrity. But you've been a great inspiration to her, and I think you'll understand why when I tell you what she said in her acceptance speech. She stood up in front of the entire publishing industry, this tiny woman, for whom the microphone had to be lowered a good deal, and in a very spontaneous way said something like this: I met numbers of you this evening, and I feel there is an intense curiosity about who I really am. Some of you who have read my book feel you know me completely. Others of you who have read the book feel I am still extremely mysterious. I think this is perhaps the right opportunity to explain a few things. I am a writer. Do you need to know anything else about me?

She said that she had been writing every day of her life for the past twenty-seven years, not knowing whether she would ever be published or not. There were times when she felt that was enough. She was a writer, and the fact that she was writing for herself and her friends and her family alone didn't matter. But there were also the days when she began to wonder if she was like the people she saw on the street talking to themselves. Was she only a crank? There were good days and there were bad days. And for twenty-seven years she had been walking this tightrope between wondering whether she was really a writer or simply a crank. And so she thanked the judges for telling her that at last she was a bona fide writer. Well, as you can imagine, that was very well received. And you can see in some of these ideas why you have been an inspiration to her. Obviously she's had a long struggle, too, and come through in blazing glory. So you're still affecting people everywhere, even Chinese-American women who live in Honolulu.

Johan [a South African who worked for the United Nations] was here for dinner tonight and he was quite despondent because a South African musical just opened in New York in which there are black performers doing native dancing and singing. Apparently it was an enormous hit in England and in Europe. But here the theater is being picketed and all the critics wrote the most vitriolic reviews, not because the show wasn't good but simply because it originated in South Africa. And I agree with him that critics are not doing their job, reviewing the play for what it is. They feel that because the performers come from South Africa they should not be singing and dancing! It's an entirely self-righteous attitude and rather deplorable. It depresses Johan greatly to come from a country which is constantly the target of such complete hatred and scorn. But we do our best to cheer him up.

You wouldn't like it here this time of year, Anaïs. I know how you dislike the cold, and it has been the most intensely cold winter — terribly low temperatures, winds, a good deal of snow. We've only been out to the country, oh, three times since early December, which is quite unusual for us. At the very beginning of December, one morning when I was wandering around the house with a cup of coffee in my hand, trying to wake up, I peered out of the window and saw a deer swimming the full length of the pond. It was a marvelous sight. And the following week the pond was frozen over completely and we were skating on it. So winter arrived that fast, and since then we've been more or less locked in with ice and snow. It's all quite beautiful, understand, but it does present certain difficulties in getting out there, and it limits what we can do once we're there, although it is pleasant to curl up by the fire and read. And I'm always diverted by birdwatching at this time of year. You feed your birds the year round, I know, but I feel that birds should work for their living when there's food available. It's enormous fun to just sit and watch them fly in and out as though it were an airport. The problem is that when we're not there the birdfeeder gets empty and we lose our whole population. They naturally go elsewhere looking for food and it takes a while before they begin to drift back again.

I see that Bob Snyder's book, *Anaïs Nin Observed*, has been published. I spotted it in our bookstore and promptly bought a copy. What do you think of it? I looked through it and it immediately made me eager to get started on our own photograph book, which I know we're going to do before too long. I think I told Rupert that we're going to sell the rights to the erotica — the paperback rights, that is — early in February. There's a great deal of interest among the mass market publishers. And we're hoping to get a handsome price for it, which ought to cheer you immensely. I'm still waiting to hear from various people who received the galleys. Henry [Miller], for example. And Larry [Durrell], as well as a number of other people. But I'm sure they'll all come through in time.

Well, I've just looked at my watch and discovered it's midnight, which is a great surprise. So off to bed. I'll talk with you tomorrow.

SHIRLEY ARIKER

I was living in Bennington when Nin was invited to speak at the
college. (I'd guess this was in 1970 or 1971). A friend who knew
Nin offered to drive her up to Bennington and combine it with a
visit with me. Both came over for a few hours, and we sat and
talked.

My memory is that Nin was simultaneously attentive and re-
mote, more like someone considering rather than participating.
She did ask questions, but they seemed disembodied. Was she
gathering material? It seemed a bit like that, even if there was little to discover, since ours was a too ordinary academic life.

My daughter Alexandra was about eighteen months old at the
time. She was napping when Nin first arrived but soon awoke.
Alexandra was a lovely and quite self-contained child; while Nin
seemed somewhat fascinated by our interaction (later confirmed
by my friend), she made no overtures toward Alexandra.

I thought the most striking thing about her was how absolutely artificial she looked. I found myself staring at her as much
as I could without being detected. Everything about her was false.
Her face was like a mask, unwrinkled to the point of being horri-
ble on a woman so clearly not young. Her face was powdered dead
white, and the powder was so thick it seemed as if it would flake
off. Her hair was jet black, which made her face all the more un-
real. This was in a Vermont winter and she was wearing a white
wool dress, a rather dramatic and simple fashion statement. Her
mannerisms were studied rather than spontaneous — in fact,

nothing about her seemed spontaneous. Her very posture and every movement were part of the design to create an effect. It was riveting.

I was young enough and "liberated" enough to find the effect distasteful, even as I felt for her valiant effort to keep age at a distance. As I think about it now, we were each watching the other.

SHARON SPENCER

The word that most profoundly and completely describes Anaïs is
courage which is variously defined by *Webster's Third New International Dictionary* (unabridged) as: (1) "The heart as the seat
of intelligence or feeling"; (2) "a proud and angry temper: high
spirit"; (3) *"mental or moral strength enabling one to venture,
persevere, and withstand danger, fear, or difficulty firmly and
resolutely"*; (4) confidence that encourages and sustains" (italics
added).

My personal relationship with Anaïs began on a Yugoslav
freighter in the middle of the Atlantic Ocean. For my doctoral dissertation I was reading *Children of the Albatross* whose back
cover portrays her holding one of Varda's collages. My then-husband, Srdjan Maljkovic, noticed her photo and exclaimed, "Oh!
I've met that woman!" As a technician in a film production lab,
Srdj had worked on Ian Hugo's films and had chatted with Anaïs
one day when she came in to pick up one of her husband's films.
Srdj remarked that she had been wearing a light purple or violet
jersey dress, very short with a small cutout piece at the midriff. It
later turned out, a remembrance verified by her California friends,
that this dress had been a gift from a famous designer. Srdj commented that maybe the dress was "a little too young for her" but
that it looked quite lovely anyway. He asked her if she was a
dancer (a natural question, considering her youthful appearance
and her poise and carriage, maintained marvelously even in later
life). She had replied, "No," that she was a writer.

Recollections of Anaïs Nin

I had actually read a portion of Anaïs's prose before meeting her. In the late 1960s a poet friend had shown me a copy of *Solar Barque*, which was later revised and integrated into *Seduction of the Minotaur*. Although I was intrigued by the fluid sensuous writing, I was much too involved with my studies and with my financial needs as a student dependent on scholarships to devote myself to further exploration of Nin's writings. Consequently, the late 1960s passed without my developing the avid hunger so many women felt for Anaïs's *Diary*. But when world-renowned authority on modern French literature, Professor Anna Balakian, my mentor at New York University, suggested that I include Nin's fiction in my doctoral study and, later, that I send Anaïs the sections of my dissertation that situated her fiction in the context of the most highly respected European writing, I did so. Nin's response was quite unexpected. I was not at all prepared for it.

It was a Sunday morning about eleven, a time I normally do not expect to receive phone calls and do not usually even answer them. But on this particular Sunday I did answer. "This is Anaïs Nin," announced the caller. I was aghast, of course, and instantly respectful. Over the telephone Anaïs's voice was soft and fragile, and seemed meek, even humble. Hesitantly, she asked me to include more about her books in my soon-to-be-published dissertation, especially what she termed her most experimental novel, *Collages*. I sensed that this request cost her an emotional effort and I immediately agreed to add a section on *Collages*. Anaïs then invited me to meet with her at her Greenwich Village apartment just south of New York University.

Because Srdj knew Anaïs was Ian Hugo's wife, so did I. Consequently, they could not hide their relationship from us, as from so many others. During the early 1970s Srdj and I and Anaïs and Hugo, often with Anaïs's close friend, the distinguished Harcourt Brace editor John Ferrone, shared some pleasant dinners in the Japanese restaurants of Greenwich Village. But at these dinners the "real" Anaïs was a ghostly version of herself. For one thing, she was undergoing treatment for cancer; for another, she was never as vibrant with Hugo as she was with other friends and loves, especially Rupert Pole, her "west coast" husband.

My first actual meeting with Anaïs was, however, private. I

will never forget the initial impact of her luminous graciousness. We met in a small sitting room graced by Varda's collages and sumptuously decorated Indian bolsters. Anaïs was resplendent in a sapphire velvet gown with trumpet sleeves. I do not remember what I wore, but we drank espresso and I gave her one of my short stories, not really expecting that she would have time to read it. The gesture was simply to give her a gift. (Later, we often exchanged dresses, both of us able to create the illusion of being taller than our actual inches.)

What was most significant about our first meeting, however, was an unspoken but shared secret communication. At this time the depth of our intuitive rapport was clear to me because I understood immediately her desire to signal to me her adult incest with her father. This is how it occurred. With what seemed to me excessive indignation, she complained that the faculty at Cornell University had refused to approve her as a guest lecturer, ostensibly because the rumor vine alleged that she had "slept with" her brother Thorvald as well as her father. She protested that the only basis for this allegation was that she had published a book titled *House of Incest*. At once I sensed that she was subtly and surreptitiously sharing this secret with me. This made psychological sense. Initially, then, the essence of my bond with Anaïs was a deep sense of grief caused by the loss of my father through divorce and my energetic effort in adult life to find him and to reestablish a relationship. I, too, had lost my father abruptly, and without explanation, at about the same age that this trauma occurred for Anaïs, and I, too, sought out my father to repair the emotional damage and to attempt to create a new bond, though not a sexual one.

Considering that both Anaïs and her father were extremely adept at seduction and considering that when their "affair" occurred, *if* it occurred (they had not seen each other for twenty years), the attraction and its daring sexual enactment should surprise no one but the psychologically faint-hearted. But, then, I am a person about whom it is often said, "I know I can tell you anything and you won't be shocked."

Consequently, with crucial energies powerfully connected, I intuited that Anaïs and her father might have been lovers. But this was only a small part of our bond. When I met Anaïs she was very ill but still enjoying the height of her fame and conducting the love affair with the world that had always been her goal in writing. She was devoting herself to the public life of a treasured, acclaimed, and widely revered artist.

In 1971 a now celebrated weekend was organized by Magic Circle Press founders and editors Adele Aldridge and Valerie Harms. I was not invited to participate. I was hurt and disturbed by the exclusion, but I tried to make up for it by inviting myself to take part in the tribute to Anaïs at the University of California at Berkeley later the same year. I was thrilled to be part of it, to find myself addressing an audience of nearly twenty-five hundred people and receiving amused laughs, of all things. This was *joyous*. The experience of addressing such a large audience and entertaining them boosted my self-confidence amazingly. Here I met many wonderful people who have become enduring friends. But, most important, I met Rupert Pole, the vibrant man who brought a youthful energy to Anaïs in her mid life and whose devoted care kept Anaïs out of the hospital and alive in their home for the last two years of her life.

When Anaïs arranged for me to be added to the program at Berkeley, she wrote that she had to share a secret part of her life with me, and that I must never let Hugo know I had met "R." Actually, Hugo had already inquired whether I had read a novel titled *La Menteuse (The Liar)*. I interpreted his question as a trap of sorts, an invitation to discuss Rupert Pole and to disclose whether I knew of his role in the life of Anaïs.

During the early 1970s I attended nearly all of Anaïs's public addresses. At one of these events I witnessed her suave and sophisticated manner of dealing with hostile confrontation. The meeting room was a small chapel on the campus of Rutgers University. During the question-and-answer period, a woman rolled up her sleeves — yes, literally — and advanced toward Anaïs with a microphone in her raised fist. She began by accusing, "You represent everything I hate. While my brother and father were working in a factory you were lounging around writing in your diary." Met with this assault, Anaïs lifted both hands and said softly, "I'm terribly sorry but I can't hear you." There was instant applause.

Later, ingenuously perhaps, Anaïs insisted that she really could not hear the woman. This is plausible because of the volume with which the assailant was making her attack. The brilliant insouciance of this manner of handling hostile aggression made a lasting impression on me, and I have utilized it myself on various occasions. However, the real fun was in observing how creative and amusing Anaïs's response was.

Having completed my dissertation which was "in press" and would be published as *Space, Time and Structure in the Modern Novel,* and having been hired to teach comparative literature at Montclair State College (now University), I decided to write an interpretive book on Anaïs's writings. At this time Oliver Evans's vastly underrated pioneering study *Anaïs Nin* was available, as was Evelyn J. Hinz's book, *The Mirror and the Garden.* Later Bettina Knapp's brilliant study appeared. Both Knapp, a critic of broad interests and incredible productivity, grounded in a university department of French literature and language, and I, a comparatist, created interpretations of Anaïs's writings that emerged from the context of the great European literature of the early twentieth century. In *Collage of Dreams* my approach was quite different from Evans's and Hinz's, because I was grounded primarily in European literature, including Anaïs's adored master, Proust. Both Knapp and I were unique in regarding Anaïs's fiction as utterly original and far ahead of its uncomprehending cultural reception. (Unfortunately, in 1996 this is still true.)

To return to the personal theme, as I grew to know Anaïs more deeply, I became aware of another deep bond beside the shared grief at being abandoned by our fathers. We were both attempting to keep our balance poised on the high wire between guilt and atonement. In May 1994, at a conference organized by the distinguished critic Suzanne Nalbantian, Anaïs's brother Joaquín Nin-Culmell stated publicly that at the end of her life Anaïs had expressed a desire for atonement. A long look at her life suggests to me that Anaïs was constantly involved in acts of atonement. Whatever Anaïs took from life she paid for lavishly. Her liberties were hard-won and ruthlessly fought for with orgies of reckless generosity. In *Ms.* a well-known woman writer described Anaïs's generosity as "professional." To me this seemed an especially mean-spirited comment, considering that the writer in question had benefited professionally from Anaïs's "professional" generosity.

Although I believe that Joaquín Nin-Culmell's concept of atonement is spiritual, mine is more psychological in its orientation. Once again, to refer to *Webster's*, atonement can mean: (1) "restoration of friendly relations"; (2) "a theological doctrine concerning the reconciliation of God and man"; (3) "reparation (as for an offense or injury)." In my view, Anaïs never stopped atoning for her amazing audacity by struggling to free other people to the same extent that she had freed herself.

Let us look at the liberties she seized. At age fifteen or sixteen she abandoned the Catholicism which meant so much to her mother. Her response to the abrupt and shocking loss of her father was the creation of her renowned diary. Later, in Queens, New York, she dropped out of school, even though she adored all forms of learning, to help her mother support the family. At twenty, while visiting her Havana relatives, she, again defying her mother, dared to elope with the austerely handsome Hugh P. Guiler. The marriage, allegedly unconsummated for two years, was a hardship in ways. She countered the sexual adversity by engaging lovers. Her most enduring and profound liaison was, of course, with Henry Miller toward whom she felt an always ambivalent devotion. With Henry's estranged wife June, Anaïs may have experimented with physical love with another woman.

Another of Anaïs's acts of courage was her early embrace of psychoanalysis, a daring commitment at the time. She first sought treatment with Parisian René Allendy, later with the brilliant renegade from Freudian orthodoxy, Otto Rank. Later still, after an unrewarding consultation with the prominent M. Esther Harding, Anaïs entered into therapy with Jungian-oriented Martha Jaeger. And later still, with the dynamic and eclectic Bavarian-born M.D. and psychoanalyst Inge Bogner.

Finally, Anaïs was a woman who dared to fulfill herself erotically, an aspiration that in a century of acclaimed "women's liberation" has brought her more severe condemnation than praise — and by whom: other women! Perhaps one explanation for many women's malice toward her is that Anaïs was ravishingly beautiful, even in her seventies. As a result of her parents' unintentional cruelty, she did not believe in her beauty. However, she knew that others did and she used it to her advantage when she could do so, as would any other woman so blessed.

Anaïs's literary gift, once it matured in the 1930s, was formidable, and it enabled her to enrich us with a body of work which can be approached over and over again without being exhausted. I began by saying that courage was the essence of Anaïs. She dreamed of herself as a dazzling and seductive woman, which she became and remained all her life. She dreamed of herself as an artist, which she was in every aspect of her life. And she dreamed of herself as a revolutionary, which she was, not politically, but in formulating her "feminine" philosophy of writing. Although I have written in other journals and in *Collage of Dreams* in intricate detail about the process that led her in the 1930s to articulate the "feminine" ideology of writing on which her mature fiction rests, I can restate the general principles here. Perhaps following an intuition of Rank's (argued in his urgently important essay titled "Feminine Psychology and Masculine Ideology"), she concluded that women wrench themselves into imitations of men not only in their personalities but also in their artistic expressions because they have failed to explore themselves deeply and have become willing participants in the mass projections that needy males use to define femininity. Thus, women instead of taking charge of defining themselves, in general collaborate with male projections of the "feminine." "Her real self is hidden and she is hiding it,"[1] proclaimed Rank. With Rank's support (until he fell in love with her), Anaïs began the effort to strike through the mask of bogus femininity and to express an authentic feminine fiction (in concept as well as style and structure), primarily in the five novels of *Cities of the Interior*. Except for her predecessors Dorothy Richardson and Virginia Woolf, Nin's effort to exhume and to articulate an authentic feminine esthetic was a unique undertaking for its time.

Based on my twenty-year intensive study of European and international literature, I believe that apart from what I wish to say later about Anaïs's courage in combating cancer and facing death, my interpretation of the reasons her novels and stories have been so unappreciated, even reviled in the United States, might carry substantial weight with the unconvinced. To begin, Anaïs is not, as Evelyn J. Hinz valiantly tried to argue in *The Mirror and the Garden,* an "American" writer. Her literary models were Rimbaud, Proust, and D. H. Lawrence, all of whom were European males of bisexual or gay sensibilities. For a brief time when she was searching for a "voice" she imitated the writing of Henry Miller, but, fortunately, this novice work has not been published; I say "fortunately" because it would give her detractors an opportunity to attack her even more ferociously than they have already done.

Anaïs is a profoundly European writer and one with great verve and experimental flair. She was not a "realist" except in the deepest psychic sense and her fiction is not intended to tell stories nor to entertain but to be a vibrant *contribution to life as experience.* In part, because her "mother" tongues were French and Spanish, she felt free to do whatever seemed inventive and exciting with English, and she did so (occasionally, but not very often, with infelicitous results). A reader of Otto Rank's *Art and Artist: Creative Urge and Personality Development* will be familiar with the essay in which he explores the origins of language. Anaïs was using language not to narrate, not to teach, not to depict, not to portray, but to invent experience for the delectation of readers willing to venture into the mysteries of her profound terrain. For such readers, it is a rich and inexhaustible kingdom, one that literally can never be totally mined because of the unimagined depths of the human psyche. A participant who is willing to — yes — "flow" with this language will always be rewarded with discoveries unsuspected, unimagined, unhinted at, and rich beyond even the most ravenous reader's imagination.

Anaïs persisted in defining herself as an artist in spite of the ridicule, discouragement and rejection, all manner of ugly responses from readers and critics who lack the clarity of intelligence to respond positively to her fiction. Even when her body was faltering, she went on writing and kept on living to the fullest experience she could summon. But Rupert Pole was there to help her, and he did so magnificently.

From autumn 1974 until her death in January 1977, Anaïs endured terminal illness with a verve that truly unnerved me. Late in December of 1976 she asked one of her close friends, "Do you think I'm dying?" After pausing and faltering, the friend replied, "I don't know. But everybody has to die some time." Anaïs retorted, stubbornly, "Well, I'm not ready yet." One of the struggles of her life was to "let go" of persons and situations that had become destructive or too burdensome to endure. Clearly, her obsession to preserve and to protect is what fired her energies as a diarist, but this obsession also condemned her to the freight of past relationships and past enmities. She experienced extreme difficulty relinquishing life itself. Her breathless capacity to be, to know, to feel, and to participate swept her to the outer boundaries of physical agony. Her terrifying appetite for life seemed to me an expression of loyalty to the people who had cared for her, especially Rupert Pole. I think she did not want him to feel that her death meant that his efforts had failed. Like other human beings, she had died.

Like everyone else, I hope to be spared a slow painful death. However, if this should overtake me, I will feel satisfied, indeed, to meet it with the intelligence and clarity that made me breathless when I was privileged to share in the dying of Anaïs's body.

Anaïs was a total genius both in life and art and an absolute master of the literary art. There should be no argument about her stature as an artist. Her courage as a woman is only one of the many reasons I love her so unconditionally. But there are also many other reasons, including her sweetness and her adorable fragility.

NOTES

1. Otto Rank, *Beyond Psychology* (New York: Dover, 1958), 251.

PHILIP K. JASON

Early in June 1971, I met Anaïs Nin for the first time. I was a twenty-nine-year-old college teacher with a brand new Ph.D. who had written a dissertation on eighteenth-century British drama, but months before the approving signatures graced my scholarly effort, I had sought out a new project — one more in keeping with my genuine reading interests of the previous ten years. Sixty-eight-year-old Nin was in the full flush of long-awaited fame. The first three volumes of her *Diary* had appeared, and the fourth was scheduled for a few months hence. Since the publication of the first volume in 1966, Nin's audience had been growing dramatically. She was busy lecturing on the college circuit and making friends among respectable academics, especially young ones and especially women.

Yet Nin still seemed more like a phenomenon buoyed by the fashions of the sixties than an established writer. Aside from an occasional mass market reprint of *A Spy in the House of Love,* Nin's fiction was kept in print by smallish Swallow Press. Her last published volume of fiction, *Collages,* had come out in 1964. The popularity of the *Diary,* I felt, was swamping out Nin's forty years of industry writing stories, novels, and the occasional foray into criticism. The time seemed ripe for a volume that would represent the range of her achievement *before* the acclaim accorded the *Diary* volumes. I hoped that such a volume, an *Anaïs Nin Reader,* would extend and solidify her audience.

On February 10, 1971 I had sent a letter to Swallow Press proposing a "single-volume sampler of Anaïs Nin's work à la the Viking *Portables* or the *Orwell Reader.*" I argued that this book would capitalize upon and extend the momentum of such efforts as the Nin newsletter and several critical studies then underway. I was "sure that such a volume would be adopted as a textbook on many college campuses." On the 14th, Durrett Wagner responded enthusiastically. He noted that Swallow already had under consideration a new edition of *Cities of the Interior* as well as a volume of criticism about Nin. Nonetheless, he urged me to provide details, which I did two days later, insisting that a book of criticism on Nin's work would be a very different and separate undertaking. I provided an outline for the *Reader.*

Receiving no answer for several weeks, I became panicky and wrote again. By April 17, Wagner answered apologetically. He had been hoping to correspond with Nin before answering me, but he hadn't yet heard back from her. Still, he considered the project desirable and urged me to query about permission fees. He also stressed the importance of Nin's own positive response to the idea. Soon after, Wagner sent me a copy of a letter dated May 4 from Evelyn J. Hinz requesting permission to quote from several Nin titles in her forthcoming study of Nin's work. Nin projects were indeed heating up.

I first wrote to Nin on May 28, introducing myself and telling the story of my infatuation with her work. By then I could report that I had written an article on *Spy* that would soon appear in *Under the Sign of Pisces: Anaïs Nin and Her Circle.* She had already heard of my project and had written a card (postmarked May 22) blessing it. However, a few days later (and before reading my letter of the 28th), Nin had been shown my proposal and other relevant letters in the Swallow offices. Her next card was far less cordial. She asserted that I didn't know the *"extent* of [her] *audience,* nor the quality of the critical essays which have appeared, the number of published articles in all languages, the masters being written, the thesis [*sic*], the fact that I was invited by students to speak at commencement at Reed College and Bennington — that *1200* persons appeared when I spoke at Harvard and gave me a 10 min. ovation before I spoke."

In this and other correspondence, Nin showed more interest in a collection of criticism than in the *Reader* idea, but she still felt the *Reader* a useful project and she understood, in her letter of June 4, why Swallow would be interested in it from a commercial point of view. While her card of May 22 graciously asked if I'd like to drop in and provided her New York address, the letter of June 4 made such a meeting seem imperative. That letter closed with a list of recent "critical studies" that were in fact book reviews. Her partisans — Daniel Stern, Deena Metzger, Karl Shapiro, Robert Kirsch — had certainly raised her public profile with enthusiastic writings, but Nin mistook these largely ephemeral notices for something far more substantial. As an academic, I knew how far off the mark she was, but I also sensed that our disagreement about her degree of acclaim could be a sore point and would have to be negotiated carefully.

Indeed, Nin took every opportunity to fill my mail with lists of her speaking invitations, awards, and distinctions. I can't be sure why she was trying so hard to make a point of impressing me with what she could just as well have called "mere facts"; I was impressed with her writing and others were impressed by her presence and her symbolic stature.

Nin remained hungry for attention even when she had it. And she was always busily involved in the fledgling critical enterprise that would shape how she would be perceived in the future. In a copy of the spring 1971 issue of *Pisces* included in one of her mailings, Nin's handwriting appears over Benjamin Franklin's enthusiastic notice of *Americans in Paris* by George Wickes: "I do not recommend this book." She appended her name to the assessment. I imagine she mailed such copies out to several of her correspondents; my subscription copy carries no such hand notation.

By the time that I was on my way to Manhattan, my excitement about meeting Nin had become tinged with fear. She did not seem ready to hear that her fame as a fiction writer was in need of a boost, and that was the whole purpose of my project and of the visit. Despite my enthusiasm for her art, we were not kindred spirits.

Before making the trip, I had been in correspondence with Richard Centing, who was to be in New York at the same time. My exchanges with Richard had actually begun in the late summer of 1970, soon after I had discovered an issue of the nearly new *Under the Sign of Pisces* in a college library. I became a subscriber and contributor almost immediately. Centing had agreed to meet me and accompany me to Nin's (more properly Ian Hugo's) apartment. With Richard along, I felt more secure: he was already safely "inside" Nin's circle. Thanks, Richard. My knees were knocking.

Nin greeted me with her unique blend of regal elegance and studied warmth. Never truly spontaneous, she had rehearsed her persona so well over the years that something like spontaneity — you could call it "virtual spontaneity" — energized her solicitations and responses. Her attire was some sort of gown, cut high at the neck but low across the back, that complemented her aristocratic, balletic gestures. She looked at least fifteen years younger than she was — and much younger than Hugo, who was still a strikingly handsome fellow. The musical intonations of her accent — she sounded to me more like a Gabor sister than a woman of French or Spanish background — were distracting at first, soothing after some familiarity.

It did not take her long to put me at ease, but it was the ease of knowing that the role I was playing was in step with her own. I was properly respectful without gushing or fawning, and we fell into a constructive dialogue about my ideas for the *Reader*. When her reservations were expressed without the nervous, haughty edge of her correspondence, I felt that I was passing whatever kind of test the meeting was. Clearly I was being interviewed; there could be no *Nin Reader* without Nin's cooperation. In spite of myself, I was letting Nin make me feel special — even powerful. Something that helped our relationship get off to a good start was that I was just beginning to have some success in literary journals with my poetry. I don't remember exactly when I made Nin aware of this or how, but I do recollect that this fact helped soften my academic edges in her eyes; Nin was somewhat mistrustful of academics, though she needed them.

The day turned unexpectedly into a screening of several of Hugo's films, so I got to see Nin on the screen as well as on the stage of the Washington Square apartment. I remember the projector being set up in the kitchen, the images projected through a portal window set in the kitchen door so that they could fill the screen in the living room. The living room itself had as central decoration highly polished and shellacked copper plates by Hugo, the very engravings that graced Nin's Gemor Press titles. I was mesmerized by this attention and by the striking, mysterious films, and I suppose that was the point of treating me to this special screening. I left intoxicated, though I'd only had a couple of glasses of wine.

On June 9, I was able to write to Durrett Wagner about the meeting, labeling it a success and claiming that Nin and I had an understanding about the scope of the enterprise. I also wrote, and must have had good reason for doing so, that Nin felt me "competent to do justice to her work in making selections." Further correspondence with Wagner and his partner concerned permissions, contracts, and working with and through Gunther Stuhlmann. One of the late stumbling blocks that Wagner and I corresponded about was his desire to use Anna Balakian's essay as the formal introduction to the *Reader*, reducing my essay to a foreword. To this day I suspect that Nin put Wagner up to this; she had great fondness for the essay and she knew that Balakian's celebrity far outshone mine. I resisted the idea, but it was the most important of several accommodations I had to make in order to keep my collaborators happy and make the *Reader* a reality. In the end, most of my plan survived.

Nin enjoyed the summer issue of *Pisces*, which included my essay on *Spy*. She made sure I was invited to the publication party for volume four of the *Diary*, and I made my appearance for that event at the Gotham Book Mart on September 30. Nin was cordial, though I was understandably on the periphery of her court that afternoon. She played her audience like few people I have ever seen, in life or in the movies. Vivacious, mobile, all smiles and eye contact and accent, Nin galvanized the second floor reception room. My review of that volume appeared in the *Washington Post* on October 4, solidifying my good standing through the remainder of the *Reader* enterprise — or almost.

Nin was not at all happy about my desire to include the story

"Sabina," which at first she had no recollection of. Eventually, she let this otherwise uncollected piece appear. However, she was adamantly opposed to the inclusion of her preface to the first edition of *Under a Glass Bell*. She had suppressed it in later editions and no longer wanted to be represented as having voiced those sentiments. I was disappointed, but having won the "Sabina" battle saw no point in jeopardizing further cooperation by being argumentative. On several occasions, including a note written in January 1972, Nin had momentary doubts about the *Reader* concept, fearing that her writing would not excerpt well. Fortunately, those fears were fleeting.

After I delivered my manuscript to Swallow in February 1972, Nin wrote (on February 19) to object strenuously to biographical sections of my introduction and to personal dates in the chronology. The letter is quite heated: "I am sorry but a Reader is not a Biography and I strongly object to being dated while the *Diary* is going on." She resents "this constant obsession with dates," which she calls "a librarian's preoccupation." Insisting that I respect her wishes in this matter, Nin forced me into some minor editing but major soul-searching. Clearly enough, Nin at this point in her life would be her only biographer. She had just turned sixty-nine. The same letter goes on to complain about the rigors of the lecture circuit, keeping up with correspondence, and dogmatic feminists who don't applaud her work.

By early April, Nin had seen my revised introduction. On April 10 she writes praising its balance and reliability, but correcting a mistake about who introduced whom to Otto Rank. Then: "I am glad you dropped the personal dates," she continues. "You are too young to realize that the American culture has always used chronology to assume that people of 90 cannot be of any value to the present, and cannot think anything useful to 1972."

By May, I was persuading Nin, at Durrett Wagner's urging, to allow a *Diary* excerpt for the *Reader*. She agreed to my suggestion of the self-enclosed story about her trip to Morocco. Also, about this time or shortly after, Balakian's essay became established as the introduction. It had been delivered on Sunday, April 30 at "Celebration: A Weekend with Anaïs Nin," coordinated by Valerie Harms and Adele Aldridge. The report on this event in the fall 1972 issue of *Pisces* lauds Balakian's paper and announces that it "will be published soon — a literary event."

Soon, the book was in its final pre-production phases and Nin's letters attended to other matters. In one letter (undated but clearly fall 1972), she asked me to express an opinion on the Swallow Press/Gunther Stuhlmann antagonism. Each felt the other was unreasonable in business dealings, and Nin wanted someone who had worked with both to help her sort things out: "the tension between them is unbearable." I told her that I had found Stuhlmann more difficult to work with, though I understood that he tried to act in her best interest.

In another letter (early November 1972), Nin offered to help me in my job search. I was at the end of my seven years at Georgetown University where tenure was not a possibility, and she was ready to send my resumé out to her contacts in academe. She also suggested that I send my review-essay on Evelyn Hinz's study, which had appeared in the June issue of the *Journal of the Otto Rank Association,* to Robert Zaller, who was then preparing his casebook on Nin. So now, with the *Reader* almost a reality, Nin and I were being mutually supportive and exchanging confidences.

On March 23, 1973, just as the book was coming into print, Nin and I met for the third time. When she gave a lecture at American University in Washington, D.C., I was in attendance. In a brief article in *Pisces* (Spring 1973), I reported on this event. As the evening wound down, Nin and I had a chance to get away from the remnants of her audience and catch up on our plans and concerns. Nin was a bit worn and far less guarded than at our first meeting or at the September book party, exchanging the platform persona she had just put on for a more intimate and more authentic self. She gave me none of the *noblesse oblige* impressions that she had in June of the previous year. We were just friends.

As such, she wrote to me excitedly on May 14, 1973, sharing the early positive reviews of the *Reader* and waxing enthusiastic over Daniel Ellsberg's freedom. She encouraged a meeting in July, but somehow that never happened. In early September, Nin wrote in outrage over Benjamin Franklin's "unjust review" in *Pisces,* announcing that she had told Richard Centing never to let Franklin review again. Franklin had been mostly complimentary, but had taken me to task for not getting some bibliographical facts straight. Nin also alerted me to the *New York Times Book Review* piece by Wallace Fowlie (September 9) and asked about my teaching situation. Near the end of the letter, she added, "We have had little time to talk together and get to know each other but at least I want you to know how pleased and proud I am of the Reader and what a good selection you made."

The next and last time I saw Anaïs Nin was at a reading, I believe in the fall of 1973, at St. John's College in Annapolis. I had just begun teaching at that other Annapolis school, and I walked over to see her. At seventy, she was wearing something white and knit and clingy. She was composed, yet one sensed an effort of will, a strain. Was she trapped in that pose? When we spoke, she once again seemed guarded — and distracted. I remembered the closing lines of her May letter — "I can see Miller was right to complain: fame means *work!*"

So Anaïs Nin left me with mixed, but powerful, impressions during the thirty months or so that we were in regular contact. She could show her imperial manner in guarded, seductive, and aloof modes. She could be engaging, protective, loyal, and generous. But she could also manifest a highly suspicious side, sensitive to possible betrayals. And she could be vehement in her denunciation of perceived betrayers, including those who would threaten her self-created world with ugly facts. She was, as she often confessed, a woman committed to and needful of illusion. To this end she could be both creative and manipulative. Such was her gift and disease.

ROCHELLE LYNN HOLT

"I walked pinned to a spider web of fantasies spun during the night, obstinately followed during the day. . . . When I ceased stepping firmly, counting my steps, when I ceased feeling the walls around me with fingers twisted like roots, seeking nourishment, the labyrinthian walk became enlarged, the silence became airy . . . and I walked into a white city."[1] This brief passage reveals how I responded to the writing of Anaïs Nin (and later to the artist in person), when as an undergraduate at the University of Illinois, in Chicago, a friend named Betty lent me the Neptunian stories which directed me to this underworld, underground literature.

Next, I read *Ladders to Fire* and was so in tune with Djuna that I was inspired to create a poem, "Let Djuna Say," which I feverishly worked on without rest for the span of seven hours. I mailed this poem to Anaïs Nin in care of her publisher. By now, I was a graduate student in the Writers' Workshop at the University of Iowa. *The Diary of Anaïs Nin* was being published by Harcourt, Brace & World when I received my first postcard from the author, dated June 2, 1969. She wrote me, "I do understand your poem and you understood Djuna. I would have written you a real letter but I am proofreading Volume 3 of the Diary, a big task, hard on the eyes. You will understand. It is good to work at linking the lines of a poem, the novel, a life. It makes a world. I'm glad you wrote me." That was the beginning of my correspondence with Anaïs, which continued sometimes on purple postcards, sometimes on ivory onionskin paper, but always handwritten in her lovely flowing script.

The first time I met Anaïs it was as though I had seen her already many times in my dreams, in the photographs of each *Diary*, or daily in my mind's eye, before that first meeting, December 3, 1971, when she invited me to read my poetry and participate in the "celebration" at Berkeley, California.

Anaïs wore two different dresses for the two days of the celebration, December 3 and 4. One was white, ivory like pearl or pure snow; the other was crimson velvet, like rich flowing blood. It was all highly symbolic to me, blood and bones, very Laurentian like Anaïs's books, mind and spirit, body and soul, a combination of what makes up a human being, and the celebration of life. The first sight of Anaïs brought tears to my eyes; she was exactly as I had pictured her in my mind, the face of an angel with a natural crown, her own auburn hair braided like an earthly halo. To me she was a collage like one of her own novels. I had heard her voice from phonograph records, but somehow it amazed me still that this was the same voice, like a bell, delicate and sweet-ringing, still very French despite her life in America. I had not imagined her tall, though, but she was, tall and thin like a model or a dancer but with petite features and small bones like an Oriental empress. Her eyes were bright like a fortuneteller's crystal, like a Spanish gypsy who has known love and sadness, pleasure and pain, the night and the day. She was childlike and very young in appearance, with complexion translucent and ethereal. At the same time she was mysterious and regal like Ishtar or Isis, and her love of the night and truth and beauty was contagious. We were all hypnotized by her words, by the sound of Anaïs, by the sight of someone we sometimes only imagined to exist. Yet here was the secret and lovely princess of Atlantis reincarnated, metamorphosed from a fish who swims through the Twelfth House most mirthfully. The evening ended with John Pearson's slides, and we joined him to "kiss the joy as it flies," the title of one of his books.

The next day I saw more of her at the celebration dinner, but I did not talk to her very much. I was shy, and she was surrounded by other people who were both part of the modern Circle and her admirers. I brought one of my own watercolors for her, "'Tis the

Woman Preying on Man's Natural Hierarchy,'' and it pleased me
when she encouraged the people at the party to come and see my
painting, to view the dancer who emerged from a plant and ate of
it at the same time, a butterfly-winged woman. Anaïs was the only
one who could have such a painting. She was quite real and yet
she could fly with transparent butterfly wings, from this world to
a more beautiful one, to brilliant and exotic dreams.

The second and last time I saw Anaïs was Saturday, December
11, 1976, the day after I had given a ninety-minute talk and slide
presentation about my private press. Deena Metzger, the director
then of the Writing Program of the Feminist Studio Workshop at
the Woman's Building in Los Angeles, had invited me to appear
on the December program coordinated by her and funded by a
grant from the Literature Division of the National Endowment
for the Arts, "In the Name of All Women." Deena drove my friend
and me up into the hills to meet Anaïs Nin and Rupert Pole. I felt
as though we were headed to a golden temple.

Her house was an Eric Wright design, described in her *Diary*,
and the spaciousness of it struck me immediately.[2] A huge glass
window-door opened onto a small pool. I noted a little goldfish
mobile I had sent with Barry Donald Jones, a gift which was dan-
gling with other windchimes. There was one clear glass pisces
fish that reflected the sunlight. Anaïs was lying in a chaise lounge,
and despite her frailty, her extreme thinness because of the cancer
and the myriad medical treatments, she was radiant in a flesh-
toned Arabian dress that matched Rupert's own caftan. A red bow
was in her golden hair to match her bright lips, and this beautiful
woman who would have been seventy-four on her next birthday
did not for a minute look her age. Her translucent Oriental complexion and sparkling eyes beamed like a young girl's. She held
my hand and called me "her daughter," told me I "was just a girl
the first time she met me" and that "now you've grown up and
become a woman." I held back my tears through that brief hour
as we sipped champagne and Anaïs reminisced, reminding us of
Isak Dinesen's penchant for oysters and champagne. She marveled that a nurse at her hospital had never heard of D. H. Lawrence, motioned to John Boyce's drawings for *Aphrodisiac* hang-

ing on her wall, and then nonchalantly pointed to the cover of her own erotica soon to be released as *Delta of Venus.*

Rupert then asked us to wait outside at the teahouse he was having built as a special birthday present for Anaïs, while he lifted her into his arms and carried her back to bed. I asked Courtenay Graham to use my camera and take a picture from outside. I regret that I did not encourage her to capture Anaïs in that special moment when we were all reunited, her face an angelic vision by the end of our meeting, but I did not want to drain her of any energy. I was glad when Anaïs said in her tiny French voice, as she left, "Some people tire me out, but not you. Not you."

I remember Anaïs propped up with pillows on her bed beneath the violet bedspread. Henry Miller's watercolors were on the wall, so vibrant and cheerful. She autographed and inscribed *Aphrodisiac* and gave me this sensual book of erotic drawings inspired by selected passages from her own work. Then she called for Deena, and I heard her ask, "Am I dying?" Deena later told us in the car that she could not tell her "Yes." I believe we knew why. Perhaps Anaïs's own words best describe Deena's answer, "No."

I thought aging meant the loss of sensibilities, of vibrations, but I feel more intensely alive than ever. Music pours freely through me, the music by which I know the extent of my receptivity and response. I thought that while parting from the dead or the dying or the sick, one parts with fragments of one's own life. I thought so many deaths would create little cemeteries in me, but I am blessed with continuous aliveness, as if on the contrary, I am to be their preserver.[3]

Anaïs Nin is still alive although she was cremated and her ashes spread over the Pacific Ocean shortly after her death on January 14, 1977; but I along with so many others she touched, her "daughters," assert her aliveness. She is with us always.

NOTES

1. Anaïs Nin, "The Labyrinth," in *Under a Glass Bell and Other*

Stories (Athens: Swallow Press/Ohio University Press, 1995), 5–6.

2. See *The Diary of Anaïs Nin, 1955–1966,* ed. Gunther Stuhlmann (New York and London: Harcourt Brace Jovanovich, 1976), 274–76.

3. Ibid., 118.

ANNA BALAKIAN

Anaïs Anaïs, time casts shadows on my memories of you. Our en-counter occurred in the last decade of your life and when my own career was struggling in mid-stream. To be personal about you means to be personal about myself as well — which is difficult for a reticent person like me; but I will give it a try at the risk of seem-ing self-serving.

It is hard to imagine two persons so unlikely to become friends and create empathy with each other and each other's work. Anaïs the free spirit, the creative firebrand, the beautiful, enchanting se-ducer of many men, worshiped by many women, the great mother of those who, losing direction in their lives, came to her with their problems and sought her solace. I, the plain and prim academic, forever trying to control inspiration by tailoring it to scholarly patterns, maintaining objectivity in writing, professional demea-nor, and distance in relationships with colleagues, sought out by students principally in career counseling and intellectual under-standing rather than for emotional affinities.

The fact is that if we had met in a social context we would never have been drawn to each other and would have remained nodding acquaintances.

It is our writings that brought Anaïs Nin and me together as well as the fact that in quite different ways we were trying to make a mark in a strictly man's world of letters. I began reading her diaries as they began to appear and was attracted by their sponta-neity and sudden but explosive insights into human character and motivations; hers were so different from the works I had read of the seventeenth-century women who engaged in epistolary writing and kept journal accounts of the French salons: stilted, studied, self-conscious. Here was verve, humor, charged capsules of images of Paris in the 1920s and 1930s. I marveled at the rapidity with which Anaïs jumped over barriers of class and ethnicities, of languages none of which she spoke or wrote flawlessly; it was extraordinary how she kept her independence and her family ties in balance, sharing her loyalty to all, battling the cavalier way her novels were treated by male novelists and poets and by critics. Seeing her as a person in the *Diary* volumes — and writing reviews of them — made me, the academic, want to put her in context. This meant reading the rest of her work, which I found directly related to my own favorite pursuit in my scholarly research and writing: the intent to prove as broadly as I could that, in the twentieth century, poetry was appropriating the form of prose to inject into it the poetic process and the analogical tempo of thought; this was true from Rimbaud forward, and had emerged as one of the most interesting facets of French surrealist writing. Anaïs Nin seemed to fit right in there among these pathblazers. She may have been a charming personality for the literati, she may have been condescendingly accepted as writer, but she was trying to do something far more serious than most critics suspected, *and they were not taking her seriously enough to notice her importance in the development of letters in our time.*

I had received word through mutual connections that Anaïs had liked my reviews and that she in turn was reading some of the rest of my critical work. The most important of these intermediaries was the poet/scholar Daisy Aldan, a former student of mine and an early enthusiast of Anaïs Nin's work. Then came an opportunity to put her officially in the context which I had discovered for her work. There was to be a two-day Anaïs Nin celebration, April 28–30, 1972, in a magnificent Westchester mansion, the Wainwright House, and admirers of hers were to express their response to her and to her work in the various dimensions of their own art. I was invited to do a "piece" on her. What I knew best to do was a scholarly study, so I spent considerable time and effort to show how her work related to that of the symbolists and surrealists, with footnotes and all. With many misgivings I drove out to Westchester, and I must have been so preoccupied with the thought that my paper might not be appropriate that in getting out of the car I left the key in the ignition but fortunately also forgot to lock the car.

That evening I became convinced that I was in the wrong place. First of all, there was only one other academic there, Elaine Marks. I confided to her that I felt very much out of place among a group of art-colony type participants — poets, painters, sculptors, novelists — and that my communication would probably be more out of place than even my person. I was ready to run away, but Elaine persuaded me to stay. The next morning I staunchly pronounced my piece. In all the years I have read papers in academe, I have never witnessed such a reception. Anaïs jumped to her feet; others became infected by her euphoria. She received my piece as if it were a pot of gold I was offering her. Why? Why? Apparently I had been the first to take her seriously in an erudite fashion. She had had other scholarly critics; the difference was that, as she explained to me later, I had put her *in the context* of the lineage of other writers, and particularly of the poets she loved.

The reason I have gone over this incident already recorded by her biographers is that it throws an important light on Anaïs's character, motivations, and frustrations. She wanted to belong to the society of men and women of letters, to the history of literature and its development. Her first book had been a critical one on Lawrence, although she had modestly called it "unprofessional" and she had written a series of critical essays assembled under the title of *The Novel of the Future*. She thought she had contributed something original in her application of psychology to fiction, but she had not been treated fairly as an avant-garde trailblazer, which she imagined she was. She suddenly had the hope that I might lead critical opinion in that direction. I was not one of the sisterhood worshiping at her feet, but some kind of torch, a mediator, toward what she had wanted from the beginning of her literary career: to be given critical recognition, to be compared to other writers, to be not only loved, but esteemed *professionally*.

Later, as we got to know each other and discussed professional matters together, we realized that we had common frustrations. There is an element of "equal rights" for women to which women who have any intellectual pretensions are particularly sensitive: to be read seriously by the literary establishment, to enter the circle of referentiality, to be accepted as contenders in the destiny of literature. To be left out of the intellectual dialogue created in both of us, in different ways, resentment and a smoldering anger, and consequently led to a strong bond between us. She accused me of not "taking care" of my work in general and particularly my most recent at the time, the first critical biography of André Breton. But without being so bold as to tell her that she had taken care of her work in the wrong way, I got an insight into some of the motivation for her much publicized erotic behavior.

The Henry Millers and Edmund Wilsons she had encountered had treated her more like the sensuous woman she appeared than as a writer to be noticed and considered critically or compared with others. In her early years she was faced with a double problem: getting published and being received as a significant writer. She solved the first problem by buying and using a printing press of her own; but as to reactions from the literati, men did not want to think about her work: they wanted to make love with her instead. Anaïs Nin puts it bluntly in speaking of her friend Peggy Glanville-Hicks, music critic of the *Herald Tribune:* "It was the first time I had heard a brilliant, effective woman demonstrate the obstacles which impaired her professional achievement because she was a woman."[1] Allusions to her own similar plight run throughout the diaries as a leitmotiv. Perhaps she sums up her situation best when she writes in 1954:

> I am not included in *New Writing* or in *Discovery*. The intellectual critics have not even read me. I am left out of magazines and anthologies. So what I feel is this: naturally I do not expect to be a popular writer, but there is a world in between, of people I want to find, who are not intellectual or political snobs, those who have feeling and intuition. . . . I want to find them, make my bridge with them. The literary poets have betrayed me. Auden asked Ruth Witt Diamant after hearing me read: "What's with Anaïs Nin?" and Ruth answered: "She is a

poet." Auden should have known this. Dylan Thomas, Tennessee [Williams], Truman Capote . . . what support did they give me?[2]

To this day, when there are so many women writers and women critics around, which ones command critical attention? It is those who are concerned with women's studies and write about the psychology of sexuality. And to go a step further, which writings about Anaïs Nin get publication support and nationwide reviews? It is those that deal with the sexual escapades with which she fattened her diaries, presumably reflecting the lifestyle she imposed on herself. I say "presumably" because my personal observations of her were not those I associate with what we old-fashioned women would call "loose" women. Let me explain.

First of all, her gratitude for that academic article — for which she managed to get wider publication by insisting that Philip Jason use it as the introduction to his anthology of her writings — was out of proportion. In fact, it is hardly ever cited or mentioned in the works and bibliographies of the many writings about Anaïs Nin which have since appeared. It was not just my *work* she liked, although that was what brought us together, and I dare say she read me more closely than most of my academic friends. But more incongruously perhaps, she liked me as a person. She was the one who called me every time she was in town; she was the one who wrote and then complained to Hugo that I had not answered her letter. Why? I was not her type; I did not flatter her. The fact is that she liked me not only for myself but for my family. She visited our home on the Upper West Side, where she met and recognized my husband as one of the cluster of "sensitive men"; she adored my children; she chose a copy of *Children of the Albatross* to inscribe for my teen-aged son, Haig, and for my daughter in her early twenties she wrote on *A Spy in the House of Love:* "Suzanne I would have loved as a daughter." She saw on our walls the paintings (worthless in the art world) containing the memories of our many family trips abroad. She loved the music we created together. In all our encounters she was accompanied by Hugo as her husband. We aroused in her a deep nostalgia for what she had missed in her own life.

Anaïs Nin's mother had been a "one-man woman," as her brother Joaquín Nin-Culmell has noted; so was I. By her father's departure Anaïs had been robbed of that family unit, and the longing for it had remained with her throughout her life, although she had ended up presenting quite a different image of her adult behavior to the world. When she was with us she had moments she lived vicariously. One of those moments occurred when she and Hugo visited us in Babylon, Long Island, where we had a cottage on the bay. With them we crossed the Captree Causeway and drove on to Robert Moses Park on Fire Island, she and Hugo arm in arm. All six of us walked on the beach, on the boardwalk. She wanted to be photographed with Hugo. It is a lovely snapshot we treasure. And she spoke of him and their early life together, softly, endearingly. As we left she said she would never forget that afternoon in the warm autumn air with no crowds, only us, as if Fire Island belonged just to this little group. She reminisced about trips she had taken with Hugo; she told us how the natural world they both loved brought them closer together. All the way back to Babylon she clung to him tightly, and when she kissed all of us goodbye, she thanked us for having taken her and Hugo into our family.

The reader of these words who knows so much more about Anaïs Nin than I knew then may think that I am either attempting to sanctify her or that Anaïs was being a hypocrite. Both inferences are wrong. I have no reason to want to whitewash her; I am not a prude — it is impossible to be one and stay in this profession — and I am not part of the current Nin enterprise. And whatever has been revealed of her personal life would not change one iota of what I have judged her work to be. She had no reason to try to endear herself to us. She already had ample proof of the warm friendship we felt for her and Hugo, and she did not need to get redundant about it. She may have had what in André Gide I had observed to be the sincerity of the moment. That is to say, something in the environment gave her a pleasure she had not experienced for a long, long time; and this woman of many roles was perhaps creating for herself the illusion of another life she might have had, and giving expression to the fact that she was enjoying it.

Another incident remains luminous out of the shadows of memory. It has to do with one of our last encounters. Hugo had invited me to have lunch with them in their Washington Square apartment. He had done the cooking, a magnificent shrimp curry. After we finished eating, we sat in Hugo's studio walled with his copper engravings, saw a few of his films, and Anaïs talked of her past and present engagements on university campuses, which she was enjoying immensely. What she loved most, she told me, were the contacts she was having with young people; she was most enchanted by their enthusiasm for her work and for her unconventional reactions to life itself. The flower children of the 1960s and 1970s somehow seemed to understand her work better than the previous generation. At one point I mentioned that I was going to Los Angeles for a lecture and would be able to get in touch with her. (She had deplored the fact that we had so much to say to each other and so few visits.) She did not answer and continued with her own stream of conversation. It happened that at a certain moment when Hugo had gone out of the room, I mentioned again my projected trip. Suddenly, her face clouded and her voice became low and almost frigid as she said: "Anna, I don't want to see you in California. You know me as the wife of Hugo; I want it to stay that way. I'll be back."

She did come back one last time into my life. In the meantime she had done more for me than I had done for her. When Hofstra University offered her the faculty medal for scholarly excellence, she told them that the gesture would be ironic unless they offered me one as well, which they promised to do and did the very next year. She gave me a set of friends I could never have had in my own university ambience: creative artists who also had respect for the scholarly approach to literature. One of these friends, Bertrand Mathieu, made it possible for me to get the Honorary Doctorate of Humane Letters at New Haven University in the company of Irving Howe. I have remained in lifelong correspondence with Mathieu who has since made his home in Rimbaud's native village in France, married one of his descendants, and fathered two children. I cherish these friends as Anaïs Nin's legacy to me, and I feel that something of her warmth and charm corresponded with theirs.

She did come back, as I said. And we met one last time in the Washington Square apartment. We talked endlessly. She wanted me to read Choderlos de Laclos, the eighteenth-century libertine author of the epistolary novel *Les Liaisons dangereuses.* The libertines in their Don Juanesque manner had subjected women to their wiles and upset the decorum of what they considered a hypocritically decadent society. Anaïs wanted me to do an article on Laclos. Suddenly, in the middle of a conversation, she stopped short and exclaimed: "Do you suppose you and I could go to Paris together one of these days, and spend a week sitting in cafés, just talking, talking. I'd like to see Paris through *your* eyes." I told her I would be thrilled. Of course the trip never took place. That conversation occurred during her last time in New York. She returned to Los Angeles to die. What is amazing is that she often mentioned her cancer, but always shook off the ominous aspect of it. Can one imagine being so desperately ill and projecting a trip to Paris? Again, the sincerity of the moment made such moments expand beyond the set dimensions of reality.

Anaïs, we were as different in lifestyle and in appearance as two women could ever be; what we shared was a certain love of literariness, which you knew you had betrayed in your pornographic writing and the then-hidden diaries because of what you attributed to "circumstances."

Part of those circumstances had to do with financial exigencies. Anaïs kept saying that people thought Hugo was rich because he worked in a bank when in fact he was a mere employee; and then once she said that the unexpurgated diaries were the "pension" she had put away for their old age. The other reason for her erotica writing was the very same one for which such excellent writers as Vladimir Nabokov in *Lolita,* Philip Roth in *Portnoy's Complaint,* and Erica Jong in *Fear of Flying* have used sexual fantasies or realities before and since her time: to gain attention, to make that initial mark on the wide market of readership. But the financial reward Anaïs hoped to get was, I think, secondary to the attention she wanted to generate for her more important writings, where she attempted to achieve the transposition of poetry into prose. Through that poetic vista she created a new perception and composition of the novel form, used psychoanalytical skills not for the purpose of dissecting personality but to discover its inner harmony. She thought that recognition for the wrong reason might lead to eventual recognition for the right reason. She thought I had brought her a step closer to the public's ultimate understanding of Anaïs Nin, the literary innovator. She felt an additional bond with me because she realized that in my own much more modest field of criticism, I too was striving for that type of recognition and knew, like her, that "women's rights" in terms of the intellect were still in arrears. Indeed, they still are. The three most significant innovators in the novel form are women: Nathalie Sarraute, Marguerite Young, and Anaïs Nin. One would not know it from the slighting they have suffered from critics or the exclusion of their work from the most recent anthologies. Of the three, Nin gets the most current exposure — but for the wrong reason. My personal impressions or feelings about Anaïs Nin are irrevocably entwined with my awareness of that injustice.

NOTES

1. *The Diary of Anaïs Nin, 1947-1955,* ed. Gunther Stuhlmann (New York: Harcourt Brace Jovanovich, 1974), 62.
2. Ibid., 164.

SAS COLBY

I remember giving Anaïs a rosebud and knowing instantly she felt beauty would have been better served by leaving the flower unpicked. She sent books with inscribed dedications to me in recycled envelopes. I would peel away the labels to learn their origins, my form of literary sleuthing. She was carefully made up, with arched eyebrows plucked in 1930s style, accentuated with a drawn line. She had the air of a European woman, confident of her appeal to men and women alike. She seemed at home in her body, moving gracefully and naturally in contrast to the artifice of her makeup. Her clothing was elegantly understated — purple was her signature color, her slim figure was clothed to her advantage. She spoke of a daily ritual, a morning swim in the nude in her pool at home in Los Angeles.

Our meeting ground was an appreciation of fantasy and a celebration of the life of the senses. Anaïs enjoyed setting and nuance. She fostered intimacy. I see her leaning forward across a table, intently in conversation. I remember her delight at finding the Welsh word *furrawn*, which means "talk that leads to intimacy."

We met at the Magic Circles' weekend at Wainwright House in Rye, New York, in 1972. I saw her perhaps four or five times from 1972 to 1975. Although I'd known about her for quite some time, I had not yet read her books. I was a young wife and mother at the beginning of a promising career as an artist, with a longing for the artistic life epitomized by Anaïs. In those early days of femi-

nism there was a sense of the possible, that we could do anything
— that we could actually live the larger lives we dreamed of. To
us, Anaïs was a model of perseverance and commitment whose
recognition had taken far too long. We felt that our time had
come at last, and drank in great gulps of freedom and expectation
with her encouragement.

In those days Anaïs was a catalyst for many in the early stages
of their artistic careers. Just as she had diagrammed her own international circle of friends in her *Diary*, her café in the sky, she now
helped form new circles by connecting the numerous acquaintances she made through her public appearances and vast correspondence. The Magic Circles' weekend brought together a diverse
group of writers and artists. I see us now arriving in the graceful
entry of Wainwright House, being greeted by Valerie Harms and
Adele Aldridge, exchanging excited introductions. A weekend in
the country, a scene updated from an Edith Wharton novel: but
the guests are Anaïs and her unconventional friends. It was as if
each person was a gift to open and discover, a treasure we would
have for life. The atmosphere was charged with the excitement of
being in the right place at the right time, a sense that anything
could happen. Although Anaïs was our reason for being there,
she refused to be the focal point and made it possible for each one
of us to tell our story in one form or another, revealing an incredible richness of talents and experience.

My art form at the time was making masks and fantasy clothing
— velvet and silk capes stitched with secret messages in inner
pockets — ritual garments that made one larger than life. My contribution to the weekend was to enact a short fantasy about happiness, out there on the lawn dancing in my masks and capes in
the spring sun with bright yellow daffodils as footlights. Anaïs appreciated the moment and wrote that my masks and capes "came
to a life of their own."[1] Her fondness for capes was well known;
the Jill Krementz photo of her caped figure was already an icon.

I found her to be extremely attentive to the people she met
through her public engagements. She welcomed all of these new
people into her life. One time she confided that she was burdened
with the correspondence this generated. People would write her
long confessional letters and she felt a need to respond in kind. I

remember suggesting that she could acknowledge their letters on a postcard. Soon after, I received a note from her on a distinctive purple postcard with a pisces logo designed for her by a friend.

Once I accompanied her on a flight from Burbank to Oakland. Rupert Pole graciously allowed me to sit next to her and warned me not to "wear her out." I told him I would do all of the talking so she could save her voice for the talk she was giving at Sonoma State. Anaïs had invited me and Susan Seddon Boulet to show slides of our artwork in conjunction with her talk on dreams. During the flight she asked about my work and I showed her a new piece called *Silky Book,* a fabric book that was inspired by meeting her. The art work was small enough for us to look at together on the plane; she showed genuine interest in exploring its hidden pockets, undoing the buttons and zippers that were activities built into the cloth pages. *Silky Book* was to be the first in a series of "artist's books," a form yet to be identified and then in its infancy. Anaïs had already commissioned me to make a velvet cape for her.

At the talk at Sonoma State (1973?) she spoke of her experience with cancer, saying that during radiation she "played movies in her head of all the good times" in her life, to help get her through the treatments. Rupert said that was the first time she'd mentioned her cancer in public. I remember her speaking on the importance of dreams to the creative process, a seamless talk, given without benefit of notes. She graciously answered questions and was entirely present and open to the moment. I did not know that her cancer had reappeared. She died four years later.

Because I was one of the few people who saw her on both coasts, she asked me not to speak of her east coast life while on the west coast, and vice versa. I assumed this was to protect her privacy and also an effort to shield her husband, Ian Hugo, in New York, from the reality of her life with Rupert Pole in Los Angeles. Although she chronicles her cross-country drive with Rupert in her published journals, along with photographs, she managed to maintain both relationships. This aspect of her life was an intriguing mystery to women of my generation who were breaking with convention to establish relationships as equals with men. We had questions, and Anaïs's life appeared to offer some answers. I say *appeared to* because although she was articulate, insightful, and responsive, I'm sure it was not her intention to offer any solutions to the dilemmas we faced as women in the 1970s, struggling to integrate a creative life with difficult economic situations, relationships, and a family life. I was not one of those who cried foul when it later became obvious there were facts and details left out of her *Diary*. There was Anaïs, and there was the myth of Anaïs, or, as some called it, the cult of Anaïs. I wanted nothing from her and was touched by her kindness at our meetings, which she invariably followed up with a written note or the gift of a book.

Although she had amazing composure and presented a dignified presence, she also had a playful humor and enjoyed a good laugh. She spoke with a French accent in a clear, fluid voice. She was clearly enjoying the recognition that had come so late in her career. I appreciated the way she responded to the feminist dialogue of the 1970s, a voice against divisive politics. Feminists wanted to call her one of their own, but I think Anaïs was beyond any kind of dogma. She generously contributed introductions and book blurbs for the publications of her many new friends.

Many of those people I met through Anaïs more than twenty years ago are at the core of my personal and artistic life today. Within three years of our meeting, my life changed by a divorce, I moved to California. Anaïs had introduced me to John Pearson, the Berkeley photographer, who in turn introduced me to Susan Seddon Boulet, the artist, who became my closest friend. John Pearson and Liz Lamson's home was "Anaïs Central" in Berkeley, a hub of activities. On the front door was a poster of Anaïs with a photograph taken by John, an expansive man who liked gathering his friends together. Dick Stoltzman, the concert clarinetist, often stayed at Liz and John's when he was in town. I made great sweeping velvet capes for them all. Later, when Anaïs was sick at the end of her life, we would call John for news of her. "She's trying an experimental treatment from Japan. She doesn't want anyone to see her like this."

Recently, musing on whether there is a contemporary cultural heroine playing a role similar to Anaïs's in the 1970s, I couldn't think of anyone. It occurred to me that as a person who is often quoted on the war between the sexes, she was a kinder, gentler Camille Paglia, but the comparison is lame. I thought of Clarissa Pinkola Estes and the popularity of her book of women's myths. Also, one can view the current interest in storytelling — in mythologizing one's personal story — in light of Anaïs's work. But there seems to be no one who provides the kind of grace and insights on the artistic life that she offered.

My involvement in books as an art form is directly related to meeting Anaïs. My current traveling exhibition, *Twenty Years of Book Thinking*, is being shown in Santa Fe, Philadelphia, and Oakland. As I write this, some former students are here helping me prepare a mailing on the Art Retreats I lead in Taos, New Mexico. One of them has a daughter named for Anaïs. And the other day Moira Collins, a cherished correspondent from the Magic Circles' weekend, called from Chicago with her new e-mail address. I'm grateful to the Anaïs connection for so many of the creative alliances and sustaining friendships in my life.

A visual memory tied to those golden California days in the 1970s is a hill covered with a tangle of wild orange nasturtiums. We spontaneously stopped the car and piled out like playful puppies so John Pearson could take our picture. Beautiful.

NOTES

1. *The Diary of Anaïs Nin, 1966–1974,* ed. Gunther Stuhlmann (New York & London: Harcourt Brace Jovanovich, 1980), 216.

VALERIE HARMS

The true meaning of my encounters with Anaïs Nin reside in my psyche. Her impact on me had to do with who I was at the time and what was needed in my development. But her impact on me is not the focus here. I am asked to describe my encounters with her. You want to hear about her and not about me. I find it difficult to tease apart the threads, following hers, not mine.

My connection with Anaïs involved three main projects: a weekend conference, a program at the New School in New York City, and the publication of her early stories.

I first heard about Anaïs Nin in a women's consciousness-raising group that met in the early 1970s. In a meeting I had described the struggle I had with writing from my personal point of view. At that time some women writers were concerned with developing a "woman's" sentence, which Virginia Woolf had suggested was important to do, considering that most published writing had been influenced by the masculine model. An artist said, "You should read Anaïs Nin." Her name was unfamiliar to me. It sounded exotic, French, romantic as well as classical.

Although my friend referred me to Anaïs's *Diary,* I first read her stories in *Under a Glass Bell,* because in order to really appreciate her, I thought I had to read her proper fiction. But it was not until reading volume one of the *Diary* that I felt impelled to write her. My idea of diaries had been based on Samuel Pepys's chronicling of what he did and saw. Anaïs described her emotional conflicts, her struggles with art, relationships, and psychoanalysis, the three topics that obsessed me, too. I was shocked — and grateful — that she revealed so much of what was on her mind. Those who later criticized her for leaving out details of her life forgot how revolutionary it was to diary literature that she included so much. But this is not the place to criticize Anaïs's critics, because that could take pages. No, suffice it to say that I wrote Anaïs a letter through her publisher, telling her that I would like to write about her.

Anaïs had written writers whom she admired and been rebuffed. She resolved to respond. A wise move, for making this effort built her circle, her café in the sky, her audience. Some, like me, were instrumental in expanding her success. She invited me to a publication party at the Gotham Book Mart for volume four of the *Diary*. It was 1972. The eighty-four-year-old Frances Steloff, founder of the Gotham, presided. I felt privileged to be there. Anaïs, who must have been the next oldest person in the room, looked the most beautiful. She wore a long, clingy velvet gown with gold lamé slippers. Her coppery hair was swept up with magenta ribbons braided through it. Composed and graceful, she signed books and spoke quietly with others.

After an exchange of letters, she invited me to visit her at Hugo's apartment in Washington Square Village. I can't begin to convey the excitement I felt at the sight of Anaïs's slanted script on a letter or purple card to me or at the prospect of meeting her. On that first visit I was accompanied by my artist friend, Adele Aldridge. Anaïs opened the door, wearing a long black dress and purple suede shoes. Her face was powdered, her eyes smudged with kohl, her lips rose. She lowered the blinds, making the room dusky and intimate. She served tea with thin slices of lemon.

Adele and I plied her with questions and revelations that most troubled our hearts. She spoke intently, as if she were considering her responses freshly. She seemed more interested in being a comrade on the path of life than a sage. She liked action as well as ideas. This — and future encounters — deeply affected our lives.

As Anaïs's reputation spread, people in Los Angeles organized a *furrawn* ("talk that leads to intimacy"), an event attended by hundreds of people. Sitting on the east coast, upset that I couldn't be there, I thought of organizing a similar event near me. When I discussed it with Anaïs, she said that she would prefer a smaller gathering, because she found large crowds overwhelming. Hence, it came about that Adele and I organized a weekend celebration at Wainwright House, Rye, New York, April 28–30, for about thirty people. The program was to center on literary friends of Anaïs. In discussion with her we decided upon Anna Balakian, the professor of literature, whose work on André Breton and surrealism was well known, and who would present a paper that was one of the best pieces of writing about Anaïs that was ever done. After Anna presented "The Poetic Reality of Anaïs Nin" to a rapt audience, Anaïs embraced her. Another person was Frances Steloff, who had given publication parties for Anaïs at the Gotham Book Mart and also discreetly held letters for her, which helped protect Anaïs's privacy. William Claire, the editor of *Voyages,* was there, also poet and publisher Daisy Aldan and sultry psychologist Beatrice Harris (who would drive Anaïs to and from the conference). Anaïs suggested that we ask Evelyn Hinz to present a critical speech. Anaïs also supplied the mailing list. Later I learned that there were people, such as Sharon Spencer, whom Anaïs had not told us about, apparently out of a wish to keep certain colleagues separate.

This stellar weekend is described and documented in the book I compiled, called *Celebration with Anaïs Nin.* The participants came from far and wide to an elegant mansion on Long Island Sound and reveled in creativity. The staff of Wainwright House, accustomed to psychological and philosophical weekends of all kinds, said that they had never seen such a high-spirited group of people.

Despite the fact that she was fighting fatigue from cancer, Anaïs was always present and responsive to manuscripts and art shoved under her door at night. She had corresponded with many of the participants and struggled to recollect their lives. She'd wanted to talk privately to individuals but felt pressured to respond to all. It is amazing to think that she was just five years from her death.

Adele said: "Anaïs is the canvas, without which the paint cannot hold. She is quiet, but it is as if she is the house, the meal, the flowers, the poetry, the garden, the cardinals, the perfume, the intimacy, and the friendships. She is the living personification of a way of being that is transmitted to everyone in the room and transformed into that separate person's essence in a real and permanent way."

Trew Bennett, a potter, said: "Anaïs has delicate, slim fingers and a lovely, smiling natural shyness, a dedication to inner beauty and expression. Her soft French accent gives a sweet richness to her, and she appears like a little girl at times. Her strength is in her vulnerability — she has the gift of great openness and this she also inspires. I sense though that she is equally private, and that she maintains this privacy in a most artful, elusive, and womanly way."

Inspired by Anaïs's Gemor Press, Adele and I started a publishing imprint called Magic Circle Press. One of our first books was about the weekend celebration. The book was produced with purple ink. We learned later that Hugo did not like the way the photographs looked; his response sounded a bit resentful about not being included (Anaïs's decision). When the book was published, we arranged a publication party at the Gotham Book Mart with Frances Steloff and Anaïs on hand. Before the party I remember Anaïs sitting and talking with a filmmaker, Frances, and us in a practical, businesslike way. She often wore a watch with a wide leather band. To me this suggested her work-oriented side that was as much a part of her as the sensuous.

I had been involved for several years with Ira Progoff's Intensive Journal program. Progoff had developed a structured journal-keeping method that had been derived from his own psychotherapy practice as well as Carl Jung's ideas about the unconscious and active imagination and D. T. Suzuki's Zen Buddhist concepts about being at one with the movement of life in a non-analytical way. In his book, *At a Journal Workshop,* Progoff mentioned his appreciation of Anaïs's use of the diary for psychoanalytical purposes. He also had written about Otto Rank. Because he and Anaïs shared some common ground, he became interested in doing a program with her. Since I knew and cared about both of them, I was enthusiastic about such an event. I thought that they would mesh harmoniously. I was naive.

The program was scheduled at the New School. Prior to the event, Ira spoke to me about wanting Anaïs to try some of his journal techniques. When I told her about that idea, she bristled (to my surprise). She said that she would certainly not do so. She had her own way and who was he to think she should serve as an example for his? She said bitingly, "We are dealing with the male ego here." I held my tongue and wondered if there would be fireworks.

The auditorium was packed. Anaïs sat demurely facing Progoff. They spoke in a general way to each other and the audience, but neither would engage with the other. They spoke about differences. The audience directed more and more questions to Anaïs. She was the star of the moment. Ira grew agitated. Afterwards he admitted that he was quite upset by the favoritism showed her. She definitely succeeded in not capitulating to his power. I realized that she had been right, and that I bowed to male authority more than I wanted to.

While I was reading all of Anaïs's books, as well as books she recommended, I was also reading her early writing, drafts that were archived at Northwestern University, on visits to my father in Chicago. Actually I was engrossed in this pursuit because of the secrets I was uncovering about Anaïs's marriage to Hugo and the sexual flavor of her relationship with Henry Miller. Mesmerizing were the preliminary drafts of *House of Incest,* and three unpublished novels, not to mention stories.

At some point it dawned on me that I could publish the stories in a special edition through my Magic Circle Press. Anaïs and I discussed the pros and cons. She did not want to see her early craftsmanship attacked by unfriendly critics; yet she was willing to be persuaded that those who were interested in her work would want a chance to read these stories as much as I had.

And so a slim book was planned. *Waste of Timelessness and Other Early Stories* had a magenta binding. Its cover design was based on a piece of fabric and stitchery by an artist (Sas Colby) who also felt indebted to Anaïs. Originally I had obtained approval from Leonor Fini to reproduce an image of hers, but when I heard that Anaïs was near death, I substituted a warm picture of her in a cameo. It turned out that Anaïs died shortly after the book was ready in 1977.

Death may end a life but not a relationship. I have since encountered Anaïs in dreams as well as dialogues on paper. Anaïs often spoke about giving birth or voice to others. Despite all that I know about her inner conflicts now, I am exceedingly grateful for all that she gave me. Her capacities for sensitivity, establishing heart-to-heart contact, and nurturing creativity are among the gifts. Her emphasis on love, beauty, literature, art, and harmonizing relationships remains unmatched.

SUZETTE HENKE

The generation of the 1960s — my generation — virtually succumbed to a love affair with Anaïs Nin. My own experience of her began first as a student in California, then during a year at the Sorbonne, when I read the diaries as they appeared in print and felt mesmerized by Nin's audacious, bohemian lifestyle and by her lyrical prose unwinding like a spool of silk thread hypnotizing the mind, enchanting the spirit, and cheering the soul. At the outset of the women's movement, Nin cast an aura around many of us hungry for independent role models. We lapped up her prose like fine, smooth wine, as we dreamily fantasized lives of hitherto unprecedented freedom, travel, and artistic creativity.

An Anaïs Nin cult took root and flourished in the 1960s California milieu, with a literary guru that appealed not only to the burgeoning flower children of that era but to women everywhere searching for revised subject-positions in the modern world. Perhaps because I had read much of her *Diary* in Parisian cafés overlooking the Seine, Nin became for me a Joan of Arc of the Left Bank (though Louveciennes was, admittedly, both geographically and socially removed from the Quartier Latin). For many of us, Nin emerged as a symbol of women's nascent liberation in love and in life — a female hero charting new creative and emotional territories for the second half of the twentieth century.

I first met Anaïs Nin at a lecture she gave at Santa Clara University in spring, 1972, when I was a doctoral student at Stanford. More than twenty years later, I can still remember her appearance onstage: she looked a bit like a princess out of a fairy tale, with long purple robes and sandalled feet. Her heart-shaped face, with its delicately chiseled features, enchanted us all. (The actress chosen to play Nin in the film *Henry and June* bears striking resemblance to Anaïs as I envisage her). Awestruck, we listened to Nin's optimistic predictions for a new era of revolutionary "sexidentities" buttressed by more egalitarian social and pyschological relationships between men and women. Having once been analyzed by Dr. René Allendy, then by Otto Rank, the mature Anaïs preached a gospel of psychoanalytic self-awareness, tempered by love and by openness to less violent and competitive social arrangements. Only a higher spiritual understanding, she insisted, would bring about a true revolution of human consciousness. Each individual, she felt, should embark on a quest to peel away false selves and expose the man, the woman, and the child in every personality. Hence her own motivation for capturing in her journals the relatively untransmuted, untransformed material of life in all its quotidian wonder.

After the lecture, I spoke with Nin about the developing field of women's studies and the place she envisioned in the university for her *roman fleuve, Cities of the Interior,* and for her ever-expanding published *Diary.* The conversations I had with her had a significant influence on my own understanding of Nin's *oeuvre,* and perhaps a subliminal effect on my intertextual interpretation of her life's work as a single body of "self-writing" that virtually transformed the fields of autobiography and confessional fiction. Understandably, Anaïs expressed a good bit of anxiety about English professors who relegated her novels to a marginal position outside the canon or dismissed her *Diary* as a hybrid genre unwelcome in the classroom. Wounded by the academic world, Nin relished her triumphant lecture tour and gloated over the obvious enthusiasm expressed by a generation of student rebels. Later, when Nin's so-called pornographic texts were released, I found myself continually on the defensive when championing her as a serious American author. "Oh, Anaïs Nin!" my colleagues would snicker. "Isn't she the obscene writer?"

In the summer of 1975, I enjoyed a brief correspondence with Anaïs Nin, who was then at the height of her international popularity. Her *Diary* had inspired and captivated a generation of women who came of age in the 1960s, and her writing was just beginning to be recognized (albeit grudgingly) by the academic establishment. The climate seemed propitious for a panel devoted to Nin at the annual meeting of the Modern Language Association, to be held in San Francisco immediately after Christmas. As a newly appointed assistant professor at the University of Virginia, I was too naive to be intimidated by the Kafkaesque procedures involved in the inauguration of MLA discussion sections, so I cheerfully set about organizing a panel of scholars to discuss Anaïs Nin's work.

It never occurred to me to consult the great woman herself, even though I had met her several years earlier. Hence my delight when Anaïs wrote to me from her home in southern California on July 17, 1975. She had heard about the project from Tristine Rainer, who had gotten the news from Dr. Lynn Sukenick. Given such third-hand information, Nin had the impression that the meeting was to be held at the Univeristy of California at Berkeley. But no matter. Not only did she applaud the endeavor, which she interpreted as a long overdue sign of scholarly recognition, but she offered to attend the session and participate as a respondent. With characteristic self-effacement, Nin meekly inquired if I "wished [her] to be there." She wanted to defend her work in person and "to be able to answer those critics who would like to attend." I was not only delighted, but felt jubilant, and told her so in a letter that now strikes me as painfully formal.

Anaïs sent me three letters over a six-month period, all originating from her southern California address. I have retained two of these letters, along with a communication from Rupert Pole and my own xeroxed responses. After Nin's initial offer to attend the MLA Convention, her second letter, dated August 2, 1975, proved more cautious. She expressed a number of compunctions about the possibility of being overwhelmed by hordes of admirers. In particular, she was "concerned about two problems," space and notoriety. "As I have given up lectures," she explained, "if you announce my coming you will be faced with a thousand students (from past experience). The big Kabuki Theatre and Palace of Art in San Francisco were not big enough!" Always a reluctant celebrity, Anaïs easily warmed to a gathering of friends and disciples; but at the first hint of criticism, she would become defensive, even prickly. She warned: "It would be best not to advertise my coming," then reiterated the admonition in more explicit terms. "Also it might be best not to make it public knowledge, as after the long 8 month bout with cancer just cured I developed a cataract in my right eye which may give me trouble and require surgery." With still a third request that I not publicize her involvement, she promised to keep in touch, concluding: "Friends and participants only will know."

What, however, did we actually know, and how much information had been left in the penumbra of Nin's lifelong masquerade? We knew that she might or might not attend the convention and participate in a discussion of her work. We knew that she had been suffering from an unnamed cancer which, apparently, had recently been cured and supplanted by less life-threatening concerns over cataracts and clarity of vision. But did Anaïs see herself, her health, and her reputation clearly at this point? Had she indeed been convinced by physicians and loved ones that the cancer was cured? Or could this have been her last masquerade, a high-spirited cheerfulness that constituted Nin's farewell gift to her family and friends? Upon receiving the August letter, I immediately tried to assure her that every effort would be made to protect her privacy.

Unfortunately, the next communication I received came from Rupert Pole, who informed me that Anaïs was far too ill to consider attending the MLA Convention. The letter, undated and entirely in capitals, reads as follows:

I FEEL I SHOULD WRITE YOU RATHER THAN ANAÏS BECAUSE ANAÏS IS ETERNALLY AND WONDERFULLY OVEROPTIMISTIC. THE CHEMOTHERAPY TREATMENTS ARE OVER BUT ALAS, NOT THEIR EFFECT. ANAÏS HAS NOT YET STARTED TO GAIN BACK THE 25 LBS. SHE LOST; IN GENERAL THE DOCTORS HAVE ADVISED ME THEY FEEL DEC. IS TOO EARLY FOR ANAÏS TO TRAVEL AND MEET WITH LARGE NUMBERS OF PEOPLE. I THINK IT WOULD BE BETTER FOR YOU TO ADVISE EVERYONE THAT SHE IS NOT COMING AND AVOID DISAPPOINTING SOME WHO MIGHT TRAVEL GREAT DISTANCES TO SEE HER. THEN, IF

SHE MAKES EXCEPTIONAL PROGRESS AND IS ABLE TO COME AT THE
LAST MINUTE —WE WILL HAVE ONLY SURPRISED, HAPPY PEOPLE.

Clearly, Anaïs was engaged in a bitter — and losing — battle
with cancer. What now strikes me as most poignant about her last
letter to me is the apparent, almost insouciant certitude with
which she dismissed her disease as "cured." Stricken with a terminal illness, Anaïs fought back with the same spirit and tenacity
that had always animated her life — and with recourse to the
mensonge vital or life-sustaining fantasy that had buoyed her up
over decades of personal and artistic struggle.

The Modern Language Association panel went forward without Anaïs, though she was definitely a pervasive presence among
us. Several of the panelists, like Sharon Spencer and Evelyn Hinz,
had been extremely close to Anaïs. Everyone seemed to know,
without daring to publicize the truth, that Nin was dying, even as
we continued our feeble attempts to propagate and immortalize
her aesthetic achievement. Noël Riley Fitch notes in her biography *Anaïs* that Nin was "honored by a special session of the Modern Language Association dedicated to her work" in December
1975. "The emerging acceptance by the academy pleases her."[1]

Now, more than two decades after my first meeting with Anaïs,
I look on her figure with the same blurred vision that character-
izes Lily Briscoe's confrontation with the ghost of Mrs. Ramsay in
Virginia Woolf's *To the Lighthouse*. She is half (step)mother
and half sister, part guardian and part seducer. Anaïs refused to be
the feminist that I would wish her to have been. To many readers
of the 1970s, Nin's autobiographical narratives seemed little more
than a meticulous anatomization of the narcissistic self — roman-
tically rebellious and creative, but dreamily detached from the
historical struggles of women in the twentieth century. It was
only in the last few years of her life that Anaïs began to develop a
nascent feminist consciousness and to associate her own marginal
plight with that of other women fighting to emerge from the
stifling cocoon of America at mid-century. Like many successful
women of that generation, she saw herself as a kind of bisexual
exception to the universal law of female oppression. I remember
her telling me that she took as her role models independent women

like Lou Andreas-Salomé, who forged their own destinies largely by gaining acceptance in traditionally male-dominated professions.

Nin's work represents one woman's battle against the stranglehold of patriarchy. She avers, somewhat naively: "I am not committed to any of the political movements which I find full of fanaticism and injustice, but in the face of each human being, I act democratically and humanly. . . . I disregard class and possessions. . . . If all of us acted in unison as I act individually, there would be no wars and no poverty."[2]

No Medea or Medusa, Nin tended to shun female anger and to redirect her frustration into elusive channels of transmutative art. By adopting an alluring stance of feminine receptivity, she manipulated her would-be masters with subversive charm, appropriating power so subtly that the mask of the ingénue rarely cracked. "I care about everything," she confesses in her *Diary.* "Emotionalism and sensibility are my quicksands."[3] Further, "I have no hatreds," she writes. "I have compassion. Everything with me is either worship, passion, or else compassion, understanding. . . . My rebellions were concealed, inhibited, indirect. . . . I don't rave against politics. I ignore it. I elect something I can love and absorb myself in it."[4] And yet, she complained of annoyance when her friends idealized her: "They all want to sanctify me, to turn me into an effigy, a myth."[5] Without politically contextualizing her efforts, Nin struggled toward the unique and isolated victories allowed by one woman's heroic self-actualization. She rebelled in a Freudian context, always believing in the illusory goals of coherent identity, psychological wholeness, and mature self-integration.

The 1992 publication of *Incest,* the unexpurgated text of the diaries that detail Nin's incestuous relationship with her long-estranged father, Joaquín Nin, forced many of us to revise the fantasy construction of the woman writer we thought we had known. In the seven published (and heavily revised/edited) diary volumes, Anaïs had given us a carefully selected, artfully crafted version of the sprawling, 150-volume manuscript that comprised her intimate life story. She had projected into the published text a luminous image of ethereal spirituality, of compassion and fragility, fortified with a powerful (narcissistic) willfulness and inner moral strength. What happens now that her readers have access to the full and sometimes shocking "truth" of her incestuous reunion with her father and her long-repressed third-trimester abortion (always delineated in diaries and short stories as a painful and traumatic stillbirth)? How does one react to the discovery that the sandalled feet of a much-admired role model might, in fact, be feet of clay?

For my part, I can only testify that having known Anaïs personally makes a substantial difference in the way I interpret her protean life-writing. In retrospect, I can criticize her narcissistic preoccupations, analyze her unresolved Oedipal attachment to her father, express shock at her incestuous relationship, and lament her submission to brutal, sometimes sadomasochistic males like Henry Miller and Gonzalo Moré. But after all such objections have been registered, I still consider Nin a heroine, of sorts, because she dared to explore the unknown territories of the female psyche with such penetrating honesty and courageous self-revelation; and because she invariably projected into any situation a totally seductive, captivating, and charismatic personality. Or was this, once again, an elusive, but convincing persona?

NOTES

1. Noël Riley Fitch, *Anaïs: The Erotic Life of Anaïs Nin* (Boston: Little, Brown, 1993), 407–8.
2. *The Diary of Anaïs Nin, 1931–1934*, ed. Gunther Stuhlmann (New York: Swallow Press/Harcourt, Brace & World, 1966), vii–viii.
3. Ibid., 11.
4. Ibid., 12.
5. Ibid., 51.

VICTOR LIPARI

The thirteen-year-old boy was already enchanted by her. He had just read the then hard-to-come-by *Tropic of Cancer* by Henry Miller, which contained a preface that she had written. Her passionate writing literally began to invade his subconscious. If Miller's book was an inspiration, her preface was a revelation to this youth, a student who wrote poetry and thought he might become a ballet dancer. That night she came to him in a dream with a beckoning, lilting, musical voice and appeared as she truly was: radiant and glowing in her pink, white, and golden aura, an illumination to him.

Twenty years later when that youngster met her face-to-face, he suddenly remembered the haunting and moving dream. Looking back on it he realized that few people like her ever come into one's life or, for that matter, into one's dreams. In the time between the dream and that actual first meeting, he had followed her now growing success and had read all the novels and all the volumes of the *Diary* that had been published. Her works, particularly the visionary *Winter of Artifice,* a collection of novelettes on the separation of a child from a parent and the subsequent reunion with that parent when an adult, had a long-lasting effect on him, since, as a boy, he had experienced this same trauma. He identified closely with the method by which she had come to terms with it through her writing. She became a constant source of enlightenment to him, enabling him to pursue the path to deeper self-discovery.

Writing was the way for him, as a man, to bring out his inner truth. As suggested in a major chapter in *The Novel of the Future*, her study of the poetic novel, he would write a book following Jung's dictum, "Proceed from the dream outward."[1] Each week he attended the creative writing class at the New School for Social Research taught by Marguerite Young, the acclaimed poet and author of *Miss MacIntosh, My Darling*, who was also the best of teachers. He began seriously to approach fiction writing. It was 1973 and, in the beginning, he had no idea that Marguerite Young was one of her closest friends. He began asking Miss Young about her and could not help but wonder if a sort of inevitable magic was bringing him a little closer to the eloquent lady. Miss Young began the countless stories about her affectionate friendship that had developed over the years with both Anaïs Nin and her husband, Ian Hugo. It was apparent that all three respected and trusted each other, sustaining a reciprocal and loyal bond.

He remembered that Ian Hugo, engraver and filmmaker, had done many illustrations, all from his original copper plates, for Anaïs Nin's books. What was he like? It was intriguing to think that Hugo was a creative artist himself and how challenging it must have been for him to work with Anaïs. Was it difficult to blend their convictions together? Marguerite Young said that Ian was the last "gentleman," the last "Scottish lord." He was regal, forthright, and noble of bearing; these attributes perhaps contributed to the couple's successful collaboration. Marguerite indicated that she would introduce the young man to them soon.

It was October 1973 and he, while still studying fiction writing and continuing to work on his novel, was employed as a clerk in a Greenwich Village bookstore. One day Anaïs Nin and Ian Hugo appeared there. Startled, he approached them and addressed them by name. Incredulous, she said, "You know me?" He replied that indeed he had avidly read and esteemed all of her works and that he was also familiar with Hugo's engravings. Immediately after this brief exchange the three of them were talking like old friends. Honey Rovit, a young writer and artist as well as a friend of the young man, also happened along; shortly thereafter, Anaïs and Hugo invited both Honey and the youth to a screening of a new movie at the Gotham Book Mart in the coming week. It was *Anaïs Nin Observed: From a Film Portrait of a Woman as Artist*, by Robert

Snyder. Honey and the young man were quick to accept, and Anaïs said she would send their invitation to the Chelsea Hotel on West 23d Street, his home at the time. It was a warm, gracious first encounter. In order not to offend Marguerite Young, who was planning a first meeting between the couple and him, he never mentioned that sunny afternoon of October 26 when the two extraordinary individuals wandered into the bookshop. When Marguerite's prearranged meeting finally occurred, the couple never mentioned it, either.

With Tom O'Horgan, the theatrical director who had mounted *Hair* and *Jesus Christ Superstar* on the Broadway stage and who had also been the director of the small but dynamic off-Broadway repertory company, the La Mama Troup, of which the young man had been an active member, and with Ericka Duncan, a young novelist, he attended the screening of *Anaïs Nin Observed*. At the legendary Gotham Book Mart he met Frances Steloff, then in her eighties. She had created it back in 1923 and was still very visible and active. On this brisk November afternoon, Anaïs arrived wearing a black cape, and since he, too, was wearing a black cape, she joked about his being a new addition to her "twins," along with Lawrence Durrell, James Leo Herlihy, and Robert Duncan. He was genuinely touched and beguiled by her remark. Anaïs, generous with her time for young artists, also got to know better Honey Rovit, Ericka Duncan, and Tom O'Horgan, as well as the young man.

Soon he was a frequent visitor at the Nin-Hugo home at 3 Washington Square Village. He would often be invited to casual screenings of Ian Hugo's films, and he developed a greater interest in both the films and Hugo's engravings. Hugo's mesmeric use of the lost art of medieval etching techniques was fascinating. Of the couple it was Ian Hugo with whom he first became close. Hugo reminded him of his own grandfather, whom he had lost some years earlier. Marguerite Young was right about the kind, optimistic, and encouraging Hugo, whom one could not help trusting and loving. Often, when Anaïs was in California and Hugo was in New York, the young man would cook for him and the two of them would spend whole evenings discussing not only Anaïs but the complexities of art and life. It was quite an education for him, and he learned that Hugo combined a practical, demanding job in banking with his pursuits of artistic self-expression. The young man realized, through Hugo's urgings, that one could not be just an artist then (or today) in America, but that one must develop other skills to satisfy one's financial needs. This was important for him because he was having difficulty balancing his practical responsibilities with his creative endeavors. Hugo always liked to mention the poet Wallace Stevens and the composer Charles Ives because they were examples of American artists who were also successful in business. Despite the difference in their ages (Hugo was in his seventies), the two friends discovered they had much in common; their friendship was an affinity for life, mutually shared. As they were seen walking about in the environs of Greenwich Village, Hugo appeared to be Dante to the young man's Virgil. The young man hoped, when Anaïs was traveling and lecturing, that Hugo, who was absolutely devoted to her and hated to be separated from her, would be less lonely, to some degree, by sharing his company. That was his wish. Hugo's new friend brought younger artists to meet Hugo, especially on the film screening evenings where a series of his films would be viewed over a glass of wine with some cheese and crackers. All the young women, including painter Mary Claire Chorba and actress Anne Louise Shirley, recognized the noble, poetic charm and wit that Hugo possessed, and they responded warmly to it. It was rejuvenating for Hugo to be with them. These evenings were memorable. When it came to his films and videos, *The Gondola Eye* stood out as the one which evoked the most excitement with a surreal vision of Venice. It remains a classic today.

During these happy times, however, Hugo told him that Anaïs was battling cancer and that she was in and out of the hospital in California. So moved to think about her suffering, the young writer suggested that there was perhaps something the two of them could do that would be of a positive nature and help to keep Anaïs's spirits up. Perhaps, the young man thought, it would be a good notion to dramatize portions of the *Diary* and the novels for a stage presentation. After all, he had already gained a wealth of experience in both theater and film while working with Tom O'Horgan and, if Anaïs agreed, he would offer to give it a try. He would write a first draft of a play about her and take it to various directors and producers whom he knew. From the beginning Hugo was happy about the plan but wanted the two of them to talk to Anaïs and see if she would subscribe to it, too. Together they telephoned her, and from her spontaneous and joyful response it appeared to be just the right idea, especially with the suggestion having come from Hugo. She was genuinely thrilled with the plan. Wanting to ease her suffering and anxiety, Hugo and the young man would create a theatrical evening that would be reassuring and, they hoped, a life-sustaining tribute to her. This was the goal. It began with Anaïs arranging for him to meet with both her Harcourt Brace Jovanovich editor, John Ferrone, and her agent, Gunther Stuhlmann. With their blessing he began "Anaïs, a Dance of Words," working feverishly on the strategy of utilizing five actor-dancers who would, in movement and words, bring six volumes (all that were published at the time) of the *Diary* to life "on the boards." With this challenging task ahead of him, he chose to use the technique of dramatic recollection: the mature actress playing Anaïs would have to review Anaïs's whole life and, in fact, create a transcendence. Having had the opportunity to review the galleys of volume seven of the *Diary,* in which Anaïs recounted her recent trip to Bali, a land where art and gentleness were revered, he had found the symbolic setting he needed. He realized that she was summing up her lifetime of struggle to blend her life as a woman with her life as an artist. Anaïs immediately understood and approved the concept when he showed her the first scenes of the play, and Hugo liked it as well. The tone was right. They discussed with him how Leslie Caron was their first choice as an actress to play Anaïs. They made such plans! Unfortunately, the play was never produced, and Anaïs soon died. Hugo was completely at sea. Trying to be of help and comfort to him during this heavy-hearted period, the young man stayed around-the-clock with Hugo for several days. Soon Joaquín Nin-Culmell, Anaïs's brother, arrived in New York to look after Hugo, who remained inconsolable. Joaquín was to become a close friend of the young man and ultimately his only link with Anaïs and Hugo, who died in 1985. Being with Joaquín today is as close to being with Anaïs and Hugo as is possible. He is of the same spirit, temperament, and artistic integrity. He has written prefaces to some of Anaïs's books and is a composer, musician, and university professor.

The last time the young man had been alone with Anaïs was perhaps the most enlightening exchange they ever had. It was sundown in New York; Anaïs was reflective and straightforward. She was able to draw him out and allow him to open his heart to her. Sitting under the collage "Women Reconstructing the World" by Jean Varda, which today hangs in his home, he talked about his mother, then dying, who had abandoned him and with whom he was later reunited as an adult. Anaïs urged him to write about her as she had done about her father in *Winter of Artifice*, advising him to focus on the love between them in all its ambivalent variations and tones.

The most important message that Anaïs had left him was this: move forward and open up more — don't hold back. Know yourself in every way and don't stop the growth, whether emotional, sexual, or spiritual. Keep opening the door to self-knowledge and awareness.

He has been trying to follow her guidance ever since.

NOTES

1. Anaïs Nin, *The Novel of the Future* (Athens: Swallow Press/ Ohio University Press, 1986), 5–23.

CHARLES RUAS

I first encountered Anaïs Nin through her work in 1967, when *The New Leader* asked me to review the first volume of her *Diary*, published by Harcourt Brace & World. I had been intrigued because when I was studying at the Sorbonne in Paris in 1963 all the girls were crazy about Anaïs's novels. I could not review the *Diary*, as I was on my way back to Europe, so I asked Fanny Howe, a young novelist, to do the assignment. When I returned to New York in the fall Anaïs was a *cause célèbre*.

I actually met Anaïs Nin in 1973, with Marguerite Young, at the Gotham Book Mart, then a center of literary life in New York City. Anaïs introduced a program of readings from Marguerite's works. I had brought Isabella Gardner and William Jay Smith, both poets, who had been great friends of Marguerite's in the days of Allen Tate.

The evening was memorable although the readings were not. The readers had been selected from Marguerite's students and were either incompetent or irritating. The exceptions were Anaïs Nin and her friend, the young actor Victor Lipari, the star of *Hair*, who was actually studying creative writing with Marguerite at the time. What remains memorable is the fact that Anaïs had arranged with Frances Steloff, the owner of the Gotham Book Mart, to host the evening for Marguerite, who was feeling very despondent after the failure of her novel *Miss MacIntosh, My Darling*, on which she had worked for twenty years and which she had hoped would rival *Ulysses*.

There could be no greater contrast than that between the world-ly elegance of Anaïs Nin and the rugged individualism of Marguerite Young. Yet there existed between them a bond of friendship, of loyalty and mutual admiration. Each had given the other clearly defined characteristics. To Marguerite, Anaïs was luminous, elegant, artistic, cultivated, wealthy, someone who led a glamorous life of adventure; she was a divided psyche always looking at herself, a Narcissus constantly in need of a reflection, gallant in her sexual adventures, a seductress, an explorer moving into new territory. Anaïs was quintessentially European in her intellectual formation and artistic sensibility. Always subjective, Anaïs was the subject of her own work.

To Anaïs, Marguerite was the uncompromising American genius, unrecognized, going her own way at her own pace, who took in everything with her encyclopedic imagination and yet wrote about everything except herself. Her work was poetic and epic, transcontinental in sweep, and centered on the heartland of this continent, in the Midwest where she was born. Marguerite's subject was the multiplicity of reality, the layering of the psyche, the conscious, the unconscious, the subconscious.

The reading at the Gotham Book Mart inspired me to contact Pacifica Radio station WBAI in New York, which was the lifeline of communication for the counterculture in those days and the center of protest against the war in Vietnam on the east coast. This was in 1973, and I was teaching at Columbia University at the time. The first program was approved, mainly on the strength of Anaïs Nin reading an introduction to the work of Marguerite Young. She extracted passages from her volume of essays, *The Novel of the Future*, and read excerpts that I would use as introductions to two programs, one on Marguerite's historical work *Angel in the Forest* and one on her novel, *Miss MacIntosh, My Darling*. As a novice, I was nervous about recording the program; by contrast, Anaïs, poised before the microphone in her flowing cape, purple floor-length gown, and lavender turban, seemed professional in her reading. I was only half conscious that the young women at the station were massing outside to catch a glimpse of their idol Anaïs through the soundproof glass window of the recording studio. Anaïs read with an accent that was neither French nor Spanish, but her voice was mellifluous and she read beautifully. These programs proved such a success that they evolved into a year-long series of readings drawn from *Miss MacIntosh, My Darling,* which I produced under the artistic direction of Rob Wynne. Various literary and theatrical figures read from chapters of the novel. During this time I was asked to become the director of arts programming at WBAI.

Soon I was initiated into the complexities of Anaïs's life. I learned that she was a trustee of Pacifica station KPFA in California, where she lived half the time. She sent me a recording she made with Rupert Pole at the West Coast station for me to broadcast in New York. Our communication was indirect, through poet Daisy Aldan, who acted as the intermediary and conveyed messages back and forth. That's when I learned that Anaïs was married to Rupert in California and led a separate existence there with a different identity. Neither Ian Hugo in New York nor Rupert knew of the other's existence, Marguerite Young told me. In California Anaïs did all the things she did not know how to do in New York. She drove a car and managed a house, was domestic and social. She was part of her husband's extensive family, she was a mainstay of the women's movement, and she was active in protesting the war in Vietnam. She and Rupert rallied support for Pacifica Radio in California.

I knew her husband Ian Hugo in New York, where I attended many evenings at their home in Greenwich Village. Ian showed us his engravings and, more important, his films of Anaïs such as *Bells of Atlantis,* which were naively surrealist, supposedly underwater portraits of Anaïs at an earlier age; the camera seemed transfixed by her beauty. At that time Anaïs sent me an excerpt from her forthcoming *Diary,* where she wrote a portrait of Marguerite Young and discussed her work. She wanted me to place it in a magazine to help promote *Miss MacIntosh, My Darling.* Anaïs wanted it to appear in *Ms.,* which was eager to have the article. I had hoped that it would appear in *Vogue* through the auspices of Leo Lerman, who was then the artistic director for Condé Nast Publications. I did not know at that time that there had been a long-standing difference between him and Anaïs. *Vogue* rejected the article, Anaïs's book came out, and it was too late for *Ms.* to use the excerpt. In my naivete I had negated Anaïs's efforts to help her friend.

Anaïs's friends always knew when she was in town because she would call when she returned, just as she called to say goodbye when she left, with unfailing courtesy and discipline. I cannot tell you how I became conscious that to many people, especially women, Anaïs represented something stellar. Beyond her fiction or her *Diary*, they wanted something from her that was intangible. I attended fundraising benefits with Anaïs for some worthy cause she championed, where I was struck by the sight of middle-aged women, behaving like teenagers, following Anaïs around the room, clinging to her clothing. For her to leave a room or depart from an event meant extricating herself from endless people and complex situations and feelings, which she invariably did with graceful aplomb. Many of the younger women were fascinated by Anaïs because they wanted to be like her — except that invariably their narcissism did not have a creative expression. Many of these devoted students became her friends and she encouraged them to become devotees of Ian Hugo and help fill the void of her absence when Anaïs was traveling, as she was forced to do more and more with her increasing fame and international reputation. Anaïs also became a leading feminist figure in Europe at this time.

I learned that Anaïs was ill with cancer because her absences became protracted and her signature purple postcards written in purple ink became less frequent. It was at this point I understood that Anaïs, who was my friend, was also a literary property to many people.

Marguerite Young had worked with Victor Lipari and Tom O'Horgan to develop her work *Angel in the Forest* into a play or filmscript. Then Victor suggested that Marguerite collaborate with Tom to write a stage drama from her novel *Miss MacIntosh, My Darling*. Marguerite threw her hopes into this project and believed that Tom would secure the backers to finance it. At all times Victor and Tom were clear and explicit about the problem of raising money for such a production, and that of necessity they would work on whichever project had funding. Marguerite had enlisted the aid of producer Edith Bel Geddes, and Tom had approached both the New York Public Theatre and Ellen Stewart at Café La Mama. When instead Café La Mama commissioned Tom and Victor to create "An Evening with Anaïs Nin," which would be autobiographical in content and based on the *Diary*, Marguerite was devastated. This meant that *Miss MacIntosh, My Darling* was suspended indefinitely while Tom and Victor devoted themselves to this new project. It was experimental theater, as Tom had several leading ladies portraying Anaïs at different periods of her life. I believe that the performance was to be called "Anaïs Anaïs," like the perfume.

The one flaw in the project was that Ian Hugo had artistic approval because Anaïs remained in California. I knew this in the back of my mind because during Anaïs's reading for the radio station, Rob Wynne had had some photos taken of her, and we were told that Ian Hugo had to approve of copies that would be used for publicity. When the time came, it was a matter of his deciding that this picture was more flattering than that one, when I could not notice any great difference. Concerning the play, however, it was a difference of artistic perspective between Ian Hugo and Tom, and the issue reduced itself to whose property Anaïs was. Victor was very close to both Tom and Ian, and everyone assumed that he would be able to surmount the differences. But he was caught between two strong personalities who would not compromise. The play was pulled from the stage a week before it was scheduled to open. No one ever saw it. That was also when we, Anaïs's friends in New York, understood that she was too ill to intercede in this matter. We even wondered if she had been too ill ever to have been told of this disastrous turn of events. It was assumed at the time that Ian Hugo had objected to amorous revelations in the production. People speculated that Tom had even gone so far in his unconventional approach as to portray Anaïs's life with Rupert in California. But all that we knew was that months of hard labor and expense by everyone involved had come to naught. All parties were crushed. Nor was Marguerite's play ever staged.

Years later I was told by Anaïs's lifelong friend Frances Field that Rupert had been Gore Vidal's lover and that they had had an argument. Gore asked Anaïs to speak to Rupert, and it turned out that she and Rupert fell in love and ran off together. Gore never forgave her. The great secret of Anaïs's life which she had withheld from the first volume of her *Diary* was that in Paris, when she was in love with Henry Miller, she had conceived his child but had decided to terminate her pregnancy. Frances was convinced that Ian had no inkling of this, but now, looking back, I think he knew everything.

Everyone had known of Anaïs's illness but no one was prepared for her death when the news reached us from California. In her obituaries she is portrayed as a seminal figure whose life and work anticipated the experimentation and freedom of the sixties and seventies. She guarded her reputation carefully, but it affected neither her nor her work. As she told her friends, fame had come to her too late and for the wrong reasons.

What remains an impressive testimony to her devotion to and respect for the artistry of Marguerite Young is the fact that shortly after Anaïs's death, her publisher, Harcourt Brace Jovanovich, made a bid for the paperback rights to *Miss MacIntosh, My Darling*. Only John Ferrone and perhaps Frances Field had known that this was Anaïs's legacy to Marguerite — keeping her work in print. The project was no doubt guaranteed by the royalties from Anaïs's work, which was a separate little industry at HBJ. *Miss MacIntosh, My Darling* was reissued as a two-volume boxed paperback set, thus making it available for another generation of readers.

By a strange irony, I had expected Anaïs Nin's reputation to increase tenfold after her death as the public learned the real story of her life, which was more interesting and stranger than even her *Diary* portrays it. But that did not happen. Her official biographer was frustrated and thwarted by the constant fight between Rupert Pole and Ian Hugo as to who really had the rights to Anaïs's story. Her subsequently published childhood diaries had an ever-dwindling audience. Slowly, her memory faded from public consciousness. It was that limbo into which famous writers fall for a period of time after their death. Now, with two biographies of her in print, Anaïs and her work await a critical reevaluation of her fiction and a definitive scholarly edition of the *Diary* that made her so famous.

ROB WYNNE

I first met Anaïs Nin about twenty years ago, in the early 1970s, when I was introduced to her by the novelist Marguerite Young. At that time I was working with Charles Ruas on a dramatization of Marguerite's book, *Miss MacIntosh, My Darling,* that Charles was producing for Pacifica Radio station WBAI in New York City. Anaïs introduced Marguerite to the listeners with a grand and quasi-psychological statement.

I remember when I first saw Anaïs that she seemed to me (to quote an unpublished remark of Gore Vidal's) rather like a half-dead lady, with lavender gums. At the time of this meeting I was just twenty, and Anaïs was in her seventies, already ill with cancer and dressed completely in purple, and shades of purple. We seemed to have an immediate rapport, and I'm sure that in some way I fell under that purple spell. I listened to and soaked up like a sponge all that she said, which seemed to me extremely theatrical, poised, and very calculated toward its effect of seduction. I had not yet read anything by Anaïs, but as I was a young artist, she very nicely gave me a copy of her book *Collages.* Coincidentally, I was at that time making a series of collages, so we seemed to have a curious bond, not really based on anything — perhaps simply a vibe.

Going back to that first meeting, we were at the recording booth of the radio station when this turbaned purple apparition appeared and spoke in what to me sounded rather like a German accent about the profound and watery effect that the prose of Marguerite Young had had on her. I remember finding it somewhat strange that this extremely famous writer was so genuinely supportive of Marguerite, who, although known and respected, did not have the following or notoriety of Anaïs. The insights and ideas Anaïs had about *Miss MacIntosh* bordered on the worshipful. There was an otherworldliness and studied mystical posture to Anaïs, as I recall. She was very lovely, rather formal, with a tender remoteness, and so baroque as to suggest to me that perhaps there was a bit of theatricality in everything that she did. I did, however, like her very much and was flattered to have the attentions of such a glamorous and unusual new friend.

As the readings progressed at the radio station, both Charles and I were invited on various occasions to Anaïs's apartment between Bleecker and Houston streets, in Greenwich Village, where her husband, Ian Hugo, quite old then, would greet us at the door elegantly dressed. By this time Anaïs was already very ill with cancer, so she would appear only for parts of these at-home evenings, where one might on occasion be treated to home movies of her in earlier years. There was such a spirit of bohemianism and exoticism and Europeanism to those evenings. All smoke and gold and dark, as I remember, and lit with candles.

As I got to know Anaïs and Ian better, I began to talk with them more as an equal. I also began to read more of the *Diary*, and I remember thinking that the theatricality that was so much a part of her presence was also in the work, that there seemed to be a planned quality, if you will, to the way the *Diary* was written. Now, I am not a literary critic, and I'm not even sure that this is a criticism, but it was something that I was definitely aware of in the work.

Also at this time I do remember a very poetic and beautiful imagist anecdote that Anaïs told me. In the 1970s, Anaïs was interested in Japan, and she had a good Japanese friend, a woman, from whom she had received a letter. When Anaïs was telling me about this letter, which had moved her deeply, she said she recalled that when she was in Japan she was served a bowl of soup, and that the soup was so exquisitely prepared and so beautiful that all she could do was weep into it, liquid into liquid; it was too lovely to eat. So you see I was increasingly carried away into this rather graceful otherworldliness of metaphor and attenuated beauty.

I also remember a party at a prominent psychiatrist's residence where all the guests, especially the women, were so happy to see Anaïs that there was a sort of queue of people waiting just to be near her. I kept thinking, what does this person see in me? After all, I was just a young artist, starting out. I had not read much of her work, or anyone else's — and perhaps that is the answer. I think that she then, as a person near the end of her life, was looking into me as if I were that bowl of soup or that pool of water into water into water. I was young and pretty and sensitive, and she was old and pretty and *very* sensitive; so this odd bond was established between us.

After I had known Anaïs for a short time in New York, she became increasingly ill and moved to California for further treatment and to spend time with Rupert Pole, whom I had heard about but never met. At this point we started an epistolary relationship and exchanged perhaps two dozen letters and postcards. All those that I received from Anaïs were extremely loving and supportive about my art and life and very flattering and tender. I cannot remember what I wrote to her. Now that I have paused to look back at our friendship, I feel that Anaïs was a unique gift, complicated and strange, and that in some perhaps unspoken way I was for her at that time a means of looking back at her youth and perhaps peeking into the unknown.

BARBARA KRAFT

I met Anaïs Nin for the first time on February 8, 1974. I know the exact date because it is the first entry in the diary I began to keep that day under her supervision. This situation came about through the auspices of International College in Los Angeles, a tutorial collegium of scholars and professionals whose roster at the time included Buckminster Fuller and Lawrence Durrell. Two and a half years later, that diary, *The Restless Spirit: Journal of a Gemini*, was published by Celestial Arts/Les Femmes with a preface by Nin.

From the moment of our initial meeting until her death a few years later I was captivated by Anaïs, who inspired intense feelings in everyone she came in contact with. No one was left indifferent by an encounter with the woman her brother referred to as the "steel hummingbird." It was either love or hate. For me it was love at first sight. Nothing I had read about Anaïs had prepared me for the experience of her which was to change the course of my life so dramatically.

When she answered the door that balmy February afternoon, the kind we Californians are known to brag about, I was mesmerized by the figure who greeted me. She was Henry Miller's "un être étoilique." Dressed in a floor-length, gauzy, cerise-hued Indian gown — a kind popular among the counterculture in those days but one which she wore regally — she was taller than I had imagined. Perhaps five feet, six inches. Her center-parted hair sat on top of her head like a tiny golden crown. There was not a line on the finely wrought, mother-of-pearl skin to indicate her seventy years. She was poetry embodied with a hauntingly accented, slightly husky, flute-like voice.

I followed in her wake as she led me into the house. She seemed to float over the rose-colored carpet like a swan skimming the surface of still water. And like a swan, which is ungainly and out of its element on firm ground, so, too, was she; but this I only came to realize years later as I reluctantly learned the facts of her life as it had been lived in contrast to her life as she had written it. I was not one of those who read between the lines of the *Diary* to the real story, perhaps because I naively thought of a diary as a relatively truthful personal revelation rather than as a literary genre.

As we sat in her small book-lined study, the shelves stacked with volumes of the *Diary* in English and various translations, our knees touching for lack of space, we discovered our "many affinities," to use her phrase. We both shared Catholic backgrounds, and musical ones, too, as I had been a pianist and "lived" in the serious music world. Our fathers had repeatedly spanked us, skirts up, over bent knees. There was our mutual interest in such women as George Sand and Lou Andreas-Salomé and more, as I was to discover over the next three years.

As the afternoon light narrowed in the room, she began to speak about her father, and she spoke of him as if he were still alive and a part of her daily existence. The plaintive, hollow timbre of her voice reminded me of the desolate sound of a metal fitting striking a flagpole in the dark swirl of night. The talk about her father made me uncomfortable. It seemed odd for a woman of her age to be revisiting the past with such pained intimacy in the company of a virtual stranger, and I felt a prick of doubt as to the stability of the woman I was about to become involved with. But I put this uneasiness quickly out of my mind for the stronger sensation was that of being transported to another world, to the realm of the possibility of things becoming. From the first I perceived her as someone unpossessible, ephemeral, forever beyond my grasp and yet someone who reached out and shook hands with my soul. There are encounters, as the Russian poet Marina Tsvetaeva once wrote, in which all that can be known is known, and this was such an encounter.[1] Implicit in our meeting was my unconditional acceptance of her as she presented herself. All those craggy places where we one day might collide were left on the doorstep of her hillside home like the rattler's shed skin. While we had many affinities, I knew even then, although I disregarded it, that we were fundamentally very different women with very different values.

And while there was utter and complete submission on my part to a superior being, there was also pity as well as love. In *Doctor Zhivago* Pasternak writes: "Occasionally we experience a deep and strong feeling. Such a feeling always includes an element of pity. The more we love, the more the object of our love seems to us to be a victim."[2] Pasternak's words aptly describe my feelings toward Anaïs, then and now. Originally these feelings were instinctive; now they live in the sad knowledge of the treacherous existence she chose for herself.

Throughout 1974 we met nearly every week, and during those sessions I would read to her from the diary that I was writing. It was the story of my life as I lived it from day to day between our meetings in the glass house overlooking Silver Lake which she shared with Rupert Pole. At the time I, too, lived in a glass house on a hill with my composer/musician husband of fourteen years and my ten-year-old daughter. Anaïs never articulated exactly what her relationship to Pole was, and I never asked. He came and went, fetched the mail, cleaned the pool, offered a glass of wine. Husband or companion? It didn't matter, and I paid scant attention to him that first year.

The tutorial relationship between Anaïs and me quickly turned into an intimacy. This gift for intimacy with those she perceived as like-spirits or would convert into like-spirits was one of her most prominent traits; and her work reverberates with references to twinship, sisterhood, and like-hood. One of the last dreams she haltingly whispered into my ear shortly before she died pictured us as twins: "I dreamed that I had all my dresses and capes laid out on the floor and that we were going to have them copied exactly for you. Then we would go out together as twins. But then someone told me that was foolish because I couldn't get up and go out and that we couldn't be twins together. And that made me feel very sad and I woke up then."

During the last week of 1974 Anaïs was hospitalized with advanced cancer. A lengthy and devastating surgery followed. For the next two years she was in and out of the hospital for repeated sessions of chemotherapy, radiation, and additional surgeries. The golden crown fell out in clumps on the bathroom floor and thereafter she was attached, through an incision on her right side, to a series of bags that drained the bilious and acidic fluids from her broken body. These years of "pain and suffering," as she referred to them, carved her a new face and rendered her a mortal being, made of flesh and bones and blood. She was felled at the very apex of her long-awaited literary success. It was a cruel blow.

Our "work" together officially stopped after a year, which ironically coincided with the onset of her illness; our intimacy, however, continued to the end of her life, as did her fervent, but embarrassing to me, admonitions that I must continue to write. It was part of Anaïs's nurturing nature to encourage creativity whenever and wherever she encountered it. And while writing was important to me, it was not the sine qua non of my existence. Praise makes me uncomfortable, and I tend, in general, to question its veracity, particularly at that time, surrounded as I was by the great talents of the music world.

As Anaïs's illness progressed, my visits became more frequent. During the last six months of her life I went to see her as often as I could, usually three or four times a week. One November night Rupert phoned me a little after 10 saying that Anaïs wanted to know if I could come to sit with her for awhile. Then he handed the phone to Anaïs and she whispered her barely audible request. When I arrived I fould her in agony. Tears streaming down her face, she asked me to get in bed with her and hold her as she could no longer bear the pain. This I did while Rupert gave her a shot of morphine. Gradually the rigid body relaxed, molding itself to mine. She drifted off to sleep in my arms like a child, her cheek wet where it touched mine. When she awoke she wept and said, "I've never done this before. I've never wept on another woman's shoulder. But there are some places where women touch that men cannot know."

Toward the end of 1976, my diary, which covers the years 1974–75, was published, exactly as it had been written and read to

Anaïs, complete with love affairs and my conflicted feelings about my husband and the future of my marriage. My husband was a member of the Los Angeles Philharmonic Orchestra and a prominent figure in Los Angeles and in the world of contemporary music nationally and internationally. Frequently we collaborated on pieces he composed which required a libretto or text. I occasionally wrote program notes for the orchestra and once appeared with it as narrator in performances of a work we had been jointly commissioned to write. The world I moved in, in those days long ago, was peopled with glamorous figures like Zubin Mehta, Pierre Boulez, Aaron Copland, Placido Domingo, Michael Tilson Thomas, Marilyn Horne and her husband, the conductor Henry Lewis, all of whom had been guests in our home.

To place these events in time, I first learned of the existence and status of Hugh Guiler (Ian Hugo) in February of 1976, some six months after I signed the contract to publish my diary, which I did with Anaïs's urgent support. The decision to publish it, of course, finally rested with me. However, Anaïs adamantly discouraged any ideas I entertained about not publishing it at all and subsequently about publishing it as a fictional work or, at the very least, under a pseudonym. She said, "Your marriage is falling apart anyway and this way you will have a book and the beginning of a new life. You will be a success. We will pick up the pieces together afterwards."

This never happened. The official book party was in November of 1976 and Anaïs died on January 14, 1977. All of this aside, I was a woman in my mid-thirties, surely an adult, who mouthed all too facilely a phrase that I still believe in, culled from a line of thinking pursued by Hannah Arendt in *The Human Condition*. To wit, action is the capacity of men to begin something new whose outcome is unpredictable. As Anaïs once told her doctors, in my presence, "Barbara did what I couldn't do. She told the truth." At the time I found her words puzzling and did not know what she meant exactly.

Had I known the consequences of my "truth," I would have had second thoughts about publishing my diary; one of them would have concerned the repercussions the book would have on my daughter and our subsequent relationship. The repercussions to my own life were harsh. I was not Anaïs Nin in her sixth decade publishing a highly distorted and tidied-up account of the life she had lived some thirty years earlier. I was a woman publishing an account of her life in the immediate present, and the doors of my world closed with celerity. There were, of course, exceptions, with Marilyn Horne, the Metropolitan Opera star and my oldest and dearest friend, being one of them. But most people who knew me perceived me as some kind of aberrant creature, a scarlet woman in their midst. There was no more smart, sophisticated life. Overnight I became a pariah in the world where I had lived for sixteen years, someone who could not be trusted. As a friend of mine observed at the time, "People don't love you for telling the truth. They hate you for it." In all likelihood I would most likely still have published my diary, but I would have done so without the illusion of affinities and instant success impairing my vision. In the end, however, the book was to become the vehicle of my freedom, and for that, I remain in Anaïs's debt. That freedom is not an easy condition and comes at a price is another issue.

For years I have struggled to come to terms with the blatant deceptions and treacherous dualities of Anaïs's life, particularly given the revelations in the posthumously published volumes *Henry and June* and *Incest.* What follows is an attempt to examine issues of meaning and accountability in the *Diary.* These are relevant issues, not only for me personally, but because Anaïs allowed herself to become a figurehead of the women's movement. "I was called out by the woman's movement to be a public figure," she states in *A Woman Speaks.*[3] In this powerful role she encouraged women to do as she had done, but she avoided any honest disclosure of the true circumstances of her life. At the many talks she gave at universities and colleges throughout the country following the highly successful publication of the *Diary,* she rhapsodized how she had created herself, how she had made her life one of meaningful growth through the creative discipline of the diary and through psychoanalysis. At these gatherings she urged women to discover themselves, to transform their lives, to free themselves from bondage, self-imposed or otherwise, as she had done. These talks, some of them edited by Evelyn Hinz and published as *A Woman Speaks,* were a siren's song. We were all encouraged to "live the dream," as she had.⁴ What we didn't know was that the dream as personified by Anaïs Nin was a nightmare of deception in moral and ethical terms. As Sissela Bok notes in *Lying,* in which she equates lying with violence as one of the two forms of deliberate assault on human beings, "deceit controls more subtly, for it works on belief as well as action."⁵

In her obsessive, nearly pathological determination to live out her unbridled dreams, Anaïs developed a rationale of "creative livingness" in which stability was the enemy. Appropriating this and other notions from D. H. Lawrence, she cut them to clothe her own dubious behavior. She supported her lies by saying that naked truth was unbearable for most people and that lies were, therefore, a more efficacious way of dealing with others. To this end she coined the grammatically incorrect phrase *"mensonges vitals,"* by which she meant the "lies which give life." In her unpublished diaries she brags about lying "bravely, ironically, dually, triply."⁶

This rhetoric, far from freeing her for "creative livingness," constricted, debilitated, and hobbled her. The last thing Anaïs had any experience of was independence or freedom. Her seemingly glamorous lifestyle was made possible by Hugh Guiler's money, and many of her books, prior to the publication of the *Diary,* were also paid for, in part or in full, by Guiler. One day, sitting in my usual chair next to the bed where she lay prostrate with the end nearing, her hand hot and dry in mine, I heard myself ask if she had known much happiness in life. "Hardly any," she whispered, turning her head to look out the window at the dank December sky.

When we read *The Diary of Anaïs Nin,* what are we reading? Fiction? Fact? Neurosis? Art? The fiction of an essentially egoless, in the Freudian sense, woman who created for herself a desperately needed, exotic Jungian persona? The chronicle of a woman who deliberately carved out a life, an identity, and succeeded in securing a place for herself in the world, the cost be damned? The story of a pathology which held its victim forever captive despite a lifetime's belief in and experience with psychoanalysis? All of the above, I would venture. She herself wrote in the 1940s that "I am giving the vision of the neurotic directly."[7]

In the face of the astounding success of her work, the *Diary* in particular, one has to address the issue of its and her popularity. What was it that compelled and continues to compel so many perfectly ordinary women to perceive of Anaïs Nin as a leader, a teacher, a spokeswoman for feminism? That she was a woman of great elegance, dignity, taste, and style was at odds with the bra-burning, let-it-all-hang-out mood of the seventies, to say nothing of the reductionist, egalitarian, combat-boot-shod nineties. Thus her appeal was and is all the more paradoxical.

By her own admission, Anaïs was not a courageous woman. She was afraid: afraid of poverty, afraid of being abandoned, afraid of aging, afraid of and unable to face life as it presents itself. This was never more evident than in one of the dreams she related to me. In the dream she was standing on top of a mountain above a waterfall that emptied into a sea below. A man in a dark suit was standing next to her, and, turning toward him, she discovered it was D. H. Lawrence. They stood there together for some time, and looking down into the water they saw Lady Chatterly swimming from ocean to ocean. "She [Lady Chatterly] was not afraid to swim in life," Anaïs said to me. "Lawrence and I were afraid to jump. We wanted to but we were not able to. We were afraid and paid a price for our fear."

Perhaps Anaïs's appeal lies precisely in the fact that she was neither a heroic nor a courageous woman, but a timorous, feminine one. There was a frailty, a poignant wistfulness about her that inspired protection despite her celebrity and the general perception of her as a superior, perfect being, a perception she went to great lengths to cultivate. While she was a woman of considerable refinement, she was not an elitist in any way. There was something very accessible about her, and this accessibility is communicated in the voice of the *Diary*. It is not a formidable, intimidating, or inflammatory voice, as were so many voices of the period. Rather it is a quintessentially feminine voice. While many women of the 1970s belligerently cast aside this part of their identity, perhaps unconsciously, they were not willing to abdicate the feminine altogether. In this sense Anaïs embodied what they had artificially rid themselves of in favor of a rhetoric. And while she gave the impression of being politically involved with the feminist issues of the day, there was concurrently a subtle communication that she had evolved to a higher level of wisdom and awareness than the rest of us, that she had, to use one of her favorite words, transcended the heated discourse of the day. By transcending the discourse, she could avoid it altogether.

We now know this was all veiled nonsense. Anaïs was not liberated. She was not self-supporting. She was not psychologically or physically free. That she continues to attract a following among the present young, the "liberated" generation of thirty-year-olds, initially surprised me, particularly since the young women I've spoken with tell me they are attracted to her work because of the sexual freedom she took for herself. This is fantastic given today's sexually liberated mores, but reveals that fundamental individual freedom can never be talked into being. It must be taken anew by each one of us, over and over again.

Equally fantastic — in the ironic sense intended by Tennessee Williams when he put it into the mouth of the defrocked Shannon in *Night of the Iguana* — is the persistent perception of Anaïs as a sexually liberated woman rather than as the disturbed individual she was. In a letter to Otto Rank she admits to not being "whole," to being crippled in the area of love. "I came to you as a cripple. You tried to live an ideal life with a cripple — to overlook the defect, the illness."[8]

Anaïs used sex for a variety of reasons, none of which — except perhaps in the case of Henry Miller, arguably the great love of her life — had much of anything to do with passion or pleasure. In the beginning her sexual escapades were a not uncommon search for her sexual being, as well as an escape from the domestic boredom, as she once told me, of Louveciennes, where tea was always served at 3 P.M. and the husband came through the gate each evening at exactly 5 P.M. As her sexual activity escalated, it evolved into a form of power and manipulation until, finally, it became a tool of her revenge.

What is the most fantastic thing of all is that so many women today, so it would seem, continue to define freedom in such a limiting manner, in such an essentially powerless arena. When there is an overabundance of anything on the market, the value of that commodity decreases proportionately. Real feminism is driven by effective action in the world through which one can attempt to achieve some degree of empowerment and definition. Action of this sort is not possible from a reclining position. It requires that one stand firmly on one's own two feet and go forward. Women who seek freedom through sexuality and define freedom as sexual promiscuity remain forever in shackles. If Anaïs's life teaches us anything, it should teach us this.

The true value of Anaïs's *Diary* lies in the candor of her feelings. Despite all the lies, the obfuscation, and the distortion of fact, what remains is the beautifully articulated expression of female feelings. Perhaps no one since George Sand had written, until Anaïs, so revealingly about the innermost emotions of women. In this expression there is veracity. I suspect a large part of women's continuing identification with Anaïs resides in the fact that her private anguish addresses a universal sense of entrapment and powerlessness that would appear to be part of the female condition. We have all experienced it at one time or another. It is a powerlessness immune, however, to rhetoric or transcendence, conquerable, in my opinion, solely by economic independence.

There is also an innocence in the chronicle of Anaïs's prolonged struggle for recognition, the innocence of the child yearning for the unattainable, that surely speaks to today's young much as it did to those of an earlier generation. It is the innocence of one who has not yet arrived, the lamentation of one who has not yet made or found a place in the world. The young of each generation are similarly on the outside looking in, striving to make their mark on the wall. Like Anaïs Nin, they have not yet entered into the work of the world. They are waiting in the wings, hopeful of a cue.

Anaïs was sophisticated and worldly, but only in respect to a limited, precious, sheltered world. She was not challenged by reality but cowed by it. In response, she erected an elaborate facade, a virtual Potemkin's Village, based on her ingenuous ideas about the power of the personal, intimate, intuitive, and transcendent. In this manner she protected herself from having to deal with the exigencies of life itself. Her days were spent in an arcane,

art-infested world divorced from the realities of everyday existence. And that was her undoing because reality finally defines
who we really are. Who was Anaïs Nin?

Her sense of herself was inextricably tied to a man's protective
presence. And the men she chose for protection, her two hus-
bands, Hugo and Rupert, were childish, gentle men. Gullible,
compliant, and steadfast, they were skillfully dominated and manipulated by her. For their part they allowed, perhaps even encouraged, her to remain forever girlish, jejune, detached from
adult responsibility and accountability. Had she been a grown-up
woman they would surely have lost her because she would have
left them both. She was aware of this and came to observe that the
diaries were, in fact, the expression of a crying, whining child. In
1953, scurrying back and forth between Hugo and Rupert, she
confides to the diary that she was "'tired of the enormous price
one pays for protection': I should have started to build up my independence long ago. The status of wife is worth nothing. If I had
worked I would be free today and not afraid to stand alone, as I
am."[9]

There is a danger in trying to know the totality of anything, of
anyone. And despite the preceding analysis I loved Anaïs, and
love is its own mystery. I did not admire her "legend" or the
woman I read about in the *Diary*. But I loved the woman in the
reality of her flesh: her beauty, her loveliness, her wistful poetry,
her reticence, her style, her pain, her suffering, her disease-
stricken voice that hovered in the air like a pale white moth.

She was a creature of artifice but she was not superficial. In
spite of everything she was a profound spirit that spoke to something in us that needs speaking to. Perhaps her greatest gift was
her power to inspire. It was implicit in her nature, a god-given
gift. One is born with such a gift; it cannot be acquired. And even
she could not totally destroy it. In her presence people felt that
they could become more, reach higher; and often they did. Long-
buried dreams and unrealized hopes rose up in the light of her
presence, often conscious for the first time. She was the physical
embodiment of poetic lyricism and in this role, the role of the
creative spirit, she spread light and hope.

Anaïs's silver dress, the one she wore for lectures and readings, still hangs in my closet. And the sun-and-moon necklace given to her by someone at the Berkeley celebration is draped over a peg on my dresser. She gave it to me that last Christmas. It was hanging on the small tree I brought and decorated for her a few days earlier. I wore both once, on that same, final Christmas day. I have never worn either of them since. They do not belong to me. They belong to her. They suit her. They *are* her.

NOTES

1. Marina Tsvetaeva, *A Captive Spirit: Selected Prose*, trans. J. Marin King (London: Virago, 1983), 115.
2. Boris Pasternak, *Dr. Zhivago*, trans. Max Hayward and Manya Harari (New York: Pantheon, 1958), 367.
3. *A Woman Speaks: The Lectures, Seminars, and Interviews of Anaïs Nin*, ed. Evelyn J. Hinz (Athens: Swallow Press/Ohio University Press, 1980), 242.
4. Deirdre Bair, *Anaïs Nin: A Biography* (New York: Putnam's, 1995), 376.
5. Sissela Bok, *Lying: Moral Choice in Public and Private Life* (New York: Vintage, 1979), 19.
6. Bair, 133, 165.
7. Ibid., 312.
8. Anaïs Nin, "Love," in *Anaïs: An International Journal* 12 (1994): 40.
9. Bair, 373.

STEPHANIE GAUPER

As with many of her readers, I became fascinated with Anaïs Nin as a person as well as a writer through her *Diary*. I have taught it for years in my women in literature classes and in classes on autobiography. Some of her novels are pleasing to me, like *The Four-Chambered Heart*, but I really believe her enduring importance lies in the *Diary*. I published two lengthy academic articles on her *Diary* in the 1980s, but never had an opportunity to see her in person until probably a year or two before her death. Though I did not know her personally, I know by accident two stories about her last days.

These stories have become increasingly important to me over the years and I consider them lessons in living and dying well. I am recovering from chemotherapy for a near death from cancer; I am engaged in writing a book on those days of all-consuming illness and recovery. I have had real occasion to meditate over Anaïs's last lessons for my life. I think experience becomes mystical as we remember and re-remember it, and maybe even remember our younger selves remembering it. Knowing Anaïs Nin as well as we often feel we do from poring over the *Diary* (her legacy of her life), we are especially affected by knowledge of her final days — her ethics and grace stood steady against the debilitating physical pain that can often bring anger and irritability.

My first story concerns her coming to lecture at Western Michigan University, where I teach. One of the professors who initially contacted her told me that Anaïs said it would be the last speaking engagement of her life — she was that ill. I don't know if that was true or not. But she was very ill, gaunt and wasted. Yet she looked absolutely splendid and carried herself regally; the word that kept coming to me was "resplendent," a grace under pressure. If memory serves me, she wore a wine-colored suit with large squared shoulder pads that kind of "bulked" her up, though her hands looked too thin, her face wan and peaked. She looked queenly. I did meet her and she was very friendly, but I doubt if she remembered me five minutes later. I know how it feels to be a speaker inundated with introductions.

What was most striking was the way she handled questions from the crowd. Many undergraduates gathered to hear her, so her audience was largely adolescents; the room was so crowded that people had to stand to hear her. She spoke briefly about some aspect of her literary career; then she opened the floor for questions. A well-meaning but brash young woman asked her to name the most difficult problems of her marriage. Anaïs smiled quietly for about thirty seconds and then leaned over the podium in the kindest fashion toward the student and said, "I will pass a hat around the room and ask every married person to drop a note in it about the worst marital problem he or she has had to deal with. Then I will hold up the hat and say, 'Yes, all of these.'" Then she did pass a hat for questions and deal directly and courageously with those that were also markedly personal. But the way she turned the first question into a lesson on decorum and universality moved me and the whole audience, too. The young woman was not humiliated; she indeed appeared to feel honored by the kindly attention from this still gorgeous and brilliant older woman. I have seen speakers who would nail such a questioner to the wall. Nin was so gentle and teaching, so generous.

The second story occurred about a year later. A young woman named Nancy called me from California. She is a nurse who had taken classes with me, knew how highly I regarded Nin's work, and had moved to California for further medical training. Nancy was already gone when the lecture described above occurred. She never called me before or after this one call; we were not particularly close. But she had been one of the nurses to care for Anaïs during the last days of her life. Nancy wanted me to know that even under the pressure of great pain, when she had to be moved, Anaïs was gracious and loving to her caregivers. Everyone loved her for her sweetness to the very end, Nancy said.

These stories matter to me because I think Anaïs's ethics of living and dying were an extension of her publication of the *Diary*. She generously shared herself in public and in the deepest privacies of dying. During the weekly chemo treatments I had for a year, I saw some nurses and doctors abused by stressed-out patients. I was sometimes worried that I could get so lost in my own pain and sickness that I would take it out on someone. I often thought of Anaïs in those days. She was able to live her ethics when it is the hardest. I hope I can follow her example. I view these stories as dharma stories that can teach us patience and loving kindness. I also think these stories embody women's ethics of caring, as Nel Noddings describes in *Caring* and Jean Bolen exemplifies in *Crossing to Avalon*. These stories tell me that living well means dying well; the fear of loss of self, of becoming unkind as death encroaches is not so overwhelming for me because of Anaïs Nin. What a marvelous human being she was.

DEENA METZGER

In the morning, I sat by Anaïs's bed and for the first time she let me hold her hand. After knocking, I had let myself into Anaïs's house without waiting for anyone to come to the door. In the past, she had opened the door graciously, wearing a long batik dress in summer, a long velvet dress in winter, and we would kiss sweetly, once on entering and again on leaving. Then we sat together on her mauve couch, a foot apart, talking, or we ran down to a restaurant near her house where we always spent more time over the menu than eating. Sometimes we ran errands together, went to the post office, the seamstress, picked up laundry, and bought tomatoes. But now she was ill, and we met differently.

Before going into Anaïs's room, I noticed the roses were tired and took them to the kitchen where I searched for a smaller vase, opening one cupboard and then another. If you can't open a cupboard and find what you need the first shot, you know you haven't been at home in a house; you have always been a guest. Among the roses were two stems of orchids, waxy, impertinent, long-living blooms. I put the orchids by themselves into a black Oaxacan vase. When it was done, I knew where everything was. I sat by Anaïs and told her that I had established my rights in her kitchen. The light flooded in, illuminating her pale face.

She said, "We've never had enough time." I could see that what remained to us depended so much upon breath. I could do little more than hold her hand, watching the light penetrate the room.

She was so thin that I saw the pillow through her fingers when the light fell on her.

After medical treatments, Anaïs's hair was very short; only a few trampled inches had returned. She had an impish look, that of a street gamin, spare and mischievous. Everything was being stripped away. The flesh dissolved and the bones shone as the fine light passed through her as through a flute.

"I've always regretted," she smiled, "not having learned to play an instrument"; and I wondered if there is a pipe one could blow with light instead of breath.

"My spirit is so light," she continued, "and this body is so heavy I cannot pick it up." To help her drink a little water, I put my hand behind her back to raise her to the cup. Later, in her sleep, she put her arms out to me and rose herself to kiss me on the lips; then she fell back.

Maybe her body was thinning to meet the spirit. Maybe she would soon be thin enough to walk again. If the body wasn't strong enough to carry its own weight, perhaps the spirit would learn to do it. When I came back the next day, she seemed heartier. Perhaps the body had reconciled itself. The gap seemed smaller; her body had more air to it; her spirit was a little denser. These were compromises, but she had more strength.

The blankets were lower on her body. She was less cold. It was not only the sun making the difference, striking her chest at an angle and radiating into a circle on her violet robe. Warmth moved slowly upwards inside her until her cheeks gleamed a little.

"You are awakening me," she put her hand out. "I've been falling asleep and waking and sleeping again, more sleep than waking. Sometimes I don't have the energy to awaken alone. When you come, it makes a difference. You pull me out."

I sat down by her, trying to appear casual. I had dressed carefully for this visit. Everything I wore had a reference to something Anaïs and I had shared. I was determined to hook her, to pull her out. The black-and-white poncho she had bought me was a setting for the black, heavy slave bracelets a black writer had given to her, authentic shackles she had sometimes worn until they became too heavy, and then she had given them to me.

I was uncomfortable in the too carefully positioned chair beside the bed. I wanted to crouch next to her, to get under the covers to snuggle as my friend Barbara Myerhoff and I did sometimes, but I felt I couldn't allow myself to sit on the bed. When I took Anaïs's hand, it fell weightless into my palm. She was so thin she stirred in the breeze from the open door like the willow tree in her garden. In the black Oaxacan vase the orchids were as sturdy as ever.

The pottery only appeared black until the light struck, and then it softened as it took the light in. Anaïs did not want anything too solid about her. The orchids air-lifted from France had survived like waxed fruit. They did not belong in her house, in that vase, on that little table covered with fragile charms and treasures, a jeweled egg, an ancient shard from Bethlehem, a fine straw pouch (smaller than her palm) filled with tiny shells. The indelicate yellow orchid petals, lined with purple veins, were too thick, too perfect, too succulent, too hardy. Not a touch of brown on the petals, not a shriveled, withered spot. Maybe they were beautiful, but in this house they absorbed all the moisture and breath. Still, I had, myself, put them in this vase knowing Anaïs, who disliked cut flowers, had become resigned to such persistent gifts; even I had brought her gardenias last summer.

"Just now as you sat by me while I was sleeping," she whispered, "I dreamed I was in a cold room and Varda — who has himself just died — entered and placed me on a marble bench." Anaïs's skin was like marble, but also it was not like marble, in the way the Oaxacan black vase was not black. In both, in the clay and the body, some heat and light remained.

"Am I dying?" Anaïs asked.

"No," I said. It was the wrong answer. I tried to correct it. "But everyone must be ready," I said.

"But I'm not ready," she whispered. Her voice was like a dry leaf. When she closed her eyes, I watched for breathing. "Breathe, Anaïs, breathe," I begged.

"I'm not ready," she said, eyes opening wide, directed toward me. "There's still so much life in me." I agreed. She was like a young girl. Outside her bedroom window was a half-finished Japanese tea house.

Holding her hands in mine, I could only bring my warmth so far. I did not know how to make a hole in Anaïs's skin for my breath to enter her as into a black clay whistle. I could bring my breath directly to her fingers, blowing as my mother had blown to warm my frostbitten hands; but Anaïs had to take the warmth from me. She had to pluck it out.

She dropped back to the pillow as if the strain of beginning the dream was too great or remembering Varda's death reminded her of her own. If Varda had not survived and he was so strapping and earthy a man. . . .

With her eyes closed, she began again, "When you and Barbara write letters each week . . . ?" Allowing her hands to remain in my palms, she momentarily slipped away. Then suddenly there was a mischievous twinkle in her eye. "I am jealous, you know," she smiled. "I never told you before, my little sister."

"Oh, you're jealous!" I didn't quite believe her but could scarcely contain my delight. "I am so pleased. Why didn't you tell me before? You're jealous! What a joy!" I wanted to snatch her from her bed, raise her up in the air, hold her in my arms above my head, twirling her frame in coronas of light. The dream of Varda waited among the orchids as I danced with Anaïs in my arms, holding her little bird body aloft. She was light as a child and she had called me "sister."

"When Barbara and I write to each other, it is like keeping a journal with two voices. But remember, Anaïs, you and I thought of beginning a correspondence long before Barbara and I began to write to each other." I reminded her that we had imagined a series of delicious lies, extravagances, conjuries, fantasies, confessions of fictional love affairs, learned references to nonexistent books, every possible romantic fraud we could conceive. We had thought of it, but had decided we were too busy and settled instead for scrawling sincere notes on plain postcards which was more serious and less time-consuming.

We did not chat; we were not extravagant with each other's time, and out of such concern we had sacrificed a thousand impromptu expressions of our love for more formal consideration of each other's obligations and commitments. To our loss we had relinquished the sloppy, spontaneous uncontainable interactions of sisters.

When Anaïs first became ill, I demonstrated my impeccable love by staying away. Each phone call and visit I contemplated but did not enact preserved, I imagined, five minutes of her solitude, an hour; they add up to days. I held myself back to give her what I thought she needed most, what one can never give another person — time. But in fact, I gave her up.

"I was jealous," Anaïs smiled again. There we were, her hand in mine, bone to bone. Then she changed her tone. "Can you tell me one of *your* dreams?" she asked.

"Do you remember when we were together a few days ago you were musing about setting up an Arab tent outside your bedroom? Well, I dreamed it for you. I walked down the beach toward the water and there, almost hidden by dunes, was a burgundy silk tent lashed with heavy sisal ropes to great wooden stakes. Even in the dream, I thought 'Anaïs sleeps here' and stood aside, marveling as the sand turned deeper, darker yellows and the sky burst into bougainvilleas."

"Then I'll have it all, won't I?" Anaïs took in the dream and leaned back into the pillows, satisfied. "I always thought we were sisters," she said. I looked at her hand, which was white, long, and narrow, lying in mine, which was thick, heavy, and broad. Mine had lines about the wrist where hers was smooth. "Look," I urged her, "of course we're sisters; we have identical hands."

She embarked on her dream again. "After Varda undressed me and laid me on the marble sepulcher, he began to paint my skin with a thousand colors and intricate designs as if I were one of his wonderful collages. And when I was completely covered, he stepped away and, levitating, I floated about the room. The transformation was beautiful; I think Varda was teaching me not to be afraid to die."

"But that's my dream," I whispered. Two months ago, I dreamed it in a different form. Victor Perera came to me, his body half painted, and asked me to cover him entirely with paisley swirls in a hundred colors. What a gift, I thought to myself, for I had not seen Victor in almost twenty years; through our meeting I had recovered part of my past.

"Perhaps, Anaïs, your dream is not about dying, but about

recovery. Write the dream down." I gave her the journal which she had hidden under her pillow.

"I'm not writing any more," she said. "I want to write about beauty, about music. I don't want to write about. . . ." Her voice broke. "You do it," she insisted.

I didn't say what I wanted to say: "Anaïs, it's life or death; you've got to write it for yourself." My words stopped as our tears often stopped when we were together. In this way, we were not good for each other.

"Yes," she cajoled, "I may write it, but you write it down as well."

That night, I dreamed that I met Anaïs in a receiving hall where she was lying down, covered with too many blankets. I tried to remove them from her but couldn't. Then I handed her a squalling child who was too much for her, and so I was forced to go away, leaving Anaïs with an admirer whom I knew was a false friend.

I understood the dream and so began to visit her more regularly, sometimes as frequently as every other day. "Come often," she said, "come every day." When I sat down by her bed, she would immediately give me her white hand. Wherever she went, I wanted to go with her. At times, we said almost nothing for the entire visit. I was afraid I did not know how to accompany her to this border.

The last time we were together, my hands were chapped and I hesitated to hold her smooth delicate hand in mine. I was afraid I'd bruise her. Two weeks later, when I was in New York, she died.

Notes on Contributors

Shirley Ariker teaches at Empire State College-State University of New York. She has a private psychotherapy practice.

Anna Balakian is former Chair of Comparative Literature at New York University. As a specialist in the field of surrealism and poetics, she has written over a hundred essays, including several on Anaïs Nin; her two latest books are *The Fiction of the Poet* and *The Snowflake on the Belfry: Dogma and Disquietude in the Critical Arena.*

Lili Bita, author and actress, is the Greek translator of Anaïs Nin's *A Spy in the House of Love.* Her ten volumes of poetry and fiction include *Furies, Firewalkers,* and *Zero Hour;* she has toured widely in her one-woman show, "The Greek Woman through the Ages."

Anatole Broyard was a longtime book reviewer for the *New York Times.* He died in 1990.

William Burford is a Fellow of the Dallas Institute of Humanities. His book of poems, *A Beginning,* was published by Norton; he recently translated and edited Proust's prefaces to Ruskin.

Since editing *Voyages,* **William Claire** has edited books on Alan Swallow and Mark Van Doren. His poems and essays have appeared in over fifty major publications, from the *Antioch Review* and *American Scholar* to the *New York Times* and *Smithsonian.*

Sas Colby is an artist and teacher whose visual work nearly always includes words and who has exhibited, lectured, and taught at international museums, universities, and craft programs. She lives in Taos, New Mexico, where she conducts summer arts retreats.

John Ferrone was on the editorial staff of Harcourt Brace Jovanovich for twenty-seven years and worked with Anaïs Nin from 1969 until her death.

Benjamin Franklin V teaches English at the University of South Carolina.

Stephanie Gauper's books include (under the name Demetrako-poulos) *Listening to Our Bodies* and *New Dimensions in Spirituality*. She teaches at Western Michigan University.

Valerie Harms is the author of eight books, most recently *The Inner Lover* and *The National Audubon Society Almanac of the Environment / The Ecology of Everyday Life*. She is also an Intensive Journal consultant and plans to be a world traveler.

Suzette Henke is Thruston B. Morton, Sr. Professor of Literary Studies at the University of Louisville. She is author of *Joyce's Moraculous Sindbook: A Study of* Ulysses, *James Joyce and the Politics of Desire*, and co-editor of *Women in Joyce*.

Rochelle Lynn Holt, like her mentor, Anaïs Nin, has been a dancer, painter, printer, sculptor, and educator. She has been writing since childhood and believes she will achieve fame earlier than Anaïs Nin and Henry Miller, if only to delight and please them.

Philip K. Jason teaches literature and creative writing at the United States Naval Academy. Among his publications are *Fourteen Landing Zones: Approaches to Vietnam War Literature* and *Anaïs Nin and Her Critics*.

Bettina Knapp teaches French and comparative literature at Hunter College and the Graduate Center of CUNY. She is the author of forty-seven books, including *Exile and the Writer, Music and the Writer, Theater and Alchemy, Antonin Artaud: Man of Vision*, and *Anaïs Nin*.

A former reporter for *Time*, **Barbara Kraft** has written fiction, poetry, plays, and essays. Anaïs Nin wrote the preface to her first book, *The Restless Spirit: Journal of a Gemini*.

Victor Lipari, member of Tom O'Horgan's original La Mama Troupe, is a writer and filmmaker. After working on the editorial staff of *Travel and Leisure* magazine for many years, he is currently completing a video biography of the Premier Danseur Noble, Igor Youskevitch.

Deena Metzger is a poet and writer whose recent books include *A Sabbath among the Ruins, What Dinah Thought*, and *Writing for Your Life*. She and Anaïs Nin had a remarkable friendship.

Lila Rosenblum is a psychotherapist. Since open-heart surgery in 1990, she has been working on her memoirs.

Gayle Nin Rosenkrantz was born in Bogota, Colombia, of Cuban-American parents, grew up in Latin America, and attended boarding school and college in the United States. She is married, has five children, practices law in San Francisco, and has been active in the environmental, peace, sanctuary, and feminist movements.

Charles Ruas is author of *Conversations with American Writers*, which contains many allusions to Anaïs Nin. He lives in New York City.

Since joining the Ohio University faculty in 1965, **Duane Schneider** has served as chair of the English Department and director of the Ohio University Press. He divides his time between Athens, Ohio, and Los Angeles.

Sharon Spencer teaches international literature at Montclair State University and is a leader in many human rights activities. She is the author of *Space, Time and Structure in the Modern Novel, Collage of Dreams: The Writings of Anaïs Nin*, two novels, over thirty short stories (including the collection *Ellis Island Then and Now*), and more than sixty review articles and essays.

Rob Wynne is an artist who lives in New York City.

Robert Zaller is Professor of History at Drexel University. He is the author of *The Parliament of 1621, The Cliffs of Solitude*, and *Lives of the Poet;* he edited *A Casebook on Anaïs Nin*.

Harriet Zinnes's recent books include *Lover* (short stories), *Blood and Feathers* (translations from the poems of Jacques Prevert), *Book of Twenty* (poems), and *My, Haven't the Flowers Been?* (poems). A literary and art critic, she is Professor Emerita of English of Queens College of CUNY.

Publications by Anaïs Nin

D. H. Lawrence: An Unprofessional Study (1932).

The House of Incest (1936).

The Winter of Artifice (1939; revised 1942; augmented 1961).

Under a Glass Bell (1944; augmented 1947; contents revised 1948; rearranged 1995).

This Hunger (1945).

Ladders to Fire (1946; shortened 1963).

Realism and Reality (1946).

Children of the Albatross (1947).

On Writing (1947).

Preface to Henry Miller's Tropic of Cancer (1947).

The Four-Chambered Heart (1950).

A Spy in the House of Love (1954).

Solar Barque (1958).

Cities of the Interior (1959; augmented 1974).

Seduction of the Minotaur (1961; augmentation of *Solar Barque*).

Collages (1964).

The Diary of Anaïs Nin, 1931–1934 (1966), ed. Gunther Stuhlmann.

The Diary of Anaïs Nin, 1934–1939 (1967), ed. Gunther Stuhlmann.

The Novel of the Future (1968).

Unpublished Selections from the Diary (1968).

The Diary of Anaïs Nin, 1939–1944 (1969), ed. Gunther Stuhlmann.

An Interview with Anaïs Nin (1970).

Nuances (1970).

The Diary of Anaïs Nin, 1944–1947 (1971), ed. Gunther Stuhlmann.

Publications by Anaïs Nin

Paris Revisited (1972).

Anaïs Nin Reader (1973), ed. Philip K. Jason.

The Diary of Anaïs Nin, 1947-1955 (1974), ed. Gunther Stuhlmann.

A Woman Speaks: The Lectures, Seminars, and Interviews of Anaïs Nin (1975), ed. Evelyn J. Hinz.

In Favor of the Sensitive Man and Other Essays (1976).

The Diary of Anaïs Nin, 1955-1966 (1976), ed. Gunther Stuhlmann.

Delta of Venus (1977; shortened as *The Illustrated Delta of Venus*, 1980).

Waste of Timelessness and Other Early Stories (1977).

Linotte: The Early Diary of Anaïs Nin, 1914-1920 (1978), trans. Jean L. Sherman.

Little Birds (1979).

The Diary of Anaïs Nin, 1966-1974 (1980), ed. Gunther Stuhlmann.

The Early Diary of Anaïs Nin: Volume Two, 1920-1923 (1982).

The Early Diary of Anaïs Nin: Volume Three, 1923-1927 (1983).

The Early Diary of Anaïs Nin: Volume Four, 1927-1931 (1985).

The White Blackbird and Other Writings (1985).

Henry and June: From the Unexpurgated Diary of Anaïs Nin (1986).

A Literate Passion: Letters of Anaïs Nin and Henry Miller, 1932-1953 (1987), ed. Gunther Stuhlmann.

Incest: From a Journal of Love: The Unexpurgated Diary of Anaïs Nin, 1932-1934 (1992).

Letters to a Friend in Australia (1992).

Conversations with Anaïs Nin (1994), ed. Wendy M. DuBow.

Fire: From a Journal of Love: The Unexpurgated Diary of Anaïs Nin, 1934-1937 (1995).

A Model and Other Stories (1995).

The Mystic of Sex and Other Writings (1995), ed. Gunther Stuhlmann.

Index

Index

Index